Guides by Skipper Bob Publications

Planning Guides –

Cruising Comfortably on a Budget. Tips on saving thousands of dollars while living and cruising on the coastal waters of the Eastern United States. How to outfit your boat and still be comfortable. ISBN 978-0-9662208-7-2 **$25**

Cruising America's Great Loop. Cruising the Great Loop up the East Coast, across the Great Lakes, down the Mississippi and Tenn-Tom Waterway to the Gulf Coast, and across the Gulf Coast to Florida. How to schedule the trip. ISBN 978-0-9662208-4-1 **$19**

Bahamas Bound. A planning guide to the Bahamas. Who should consider going. What type of vessel. How to outfit your vessel for the Bahamas to save money and enjoy the trip. Marina prices and contact information. ISBN 978-0-9662208-9-6 **$16**

Cruising Guides –

Anchorages Along The Intracoastal Waterway. Anchorages, free docks, bridge restrictions and waterway concerns from the Hudson River to Key West including the Okeechobee Waterway and St. Johns River. ISBN 978-0-9662208-3-4 **$17**

Marinas Along The Intracoastal Waterway. Fuel prices, transient slip fees, courtesy cars, long-term slip fees, do-it-yourself yards, marina facilities, monthly rates, and haul out fees from the Hudson River to Key West. ISBN 978-0-9662208-0-3 **$15**

Cruising the Gulf Coast. Cruising the Gulf Coast on the Gulf Intracoastal Waterway from Brownsville, TX to Flamingo, FL. Covers the waterway, anchorages, bridge and lock restrictions, marinas, and shopping along the way. ISBN 978-0-9727501-4-1 **$16**

Cruising the New York Canal System. Depth and height restrictions. Lock locations and characteristics. Places to stay at no charge with water and electric. Includes the Erie, Oswego, Cayuga-Seneca, and Champlain Canals. ISBN 978-0-9662208-5-8 **$15**

Cruising the Rideau and Richelieu Canals. How to plan a cruise of the historic waterways in Canada that include the Rideau Canal, Ottawa, St Lawrence River, Montreal, Quebec, Richelieu Canal, Chambly Canal, and Lake Champlain. ISBN 978-0-9662208-6-5 **$15**

Cruising the Trent-Severn Canal, Georgian Bay and North Channel. Cruising the Trent-Severn Canal including fees, services available, where to stay, etc. Includes highlights of Georgian Bay, North Channel and northern Lake Huron. ISBN 978-0-9662208-8-9 **$15**

Cruising from Chicago to Mobile. Cruising the Inland River System from Chicago to Mobile, AL on Mobile Bay. Information on anchorages, free docks, marinas, bridge and lock restrictions, and navigational concerns for this route. ISBN 978-0-9727501-5-8 **$16**

Ordering Skipper Bob Publications

Waterway Guide Ship Store – Phone 800-233-3359, ext. 1#, Internet - www.waterwayguide.com
Email booksales@waterwayguide.com

Bluewater Books & Charts – 3233 SW 2nd Avenue, Fort Lauderdale, FL 33315
Phone 800-942-2583. Internet - www.bluewaterweb.com.

Defender Industries – 42 Great Neck Road, Waterford, CT 06385
Phone 800-628-8225. Internet – www.defender.com.

Landfall Navigation® – 151 Harvard Avenue, Stamford, CT 06902
Phone 800-941-2219. Internet - www.landfallnavigation.com/skipperbob.html.

Maryland Nautical Sales – 1400 E. Clement St., Baltimore, MD 21230
Phone 800-596-7245. Internet – www.mdnautical.com.

The Nautical Mind Bookstore – 249 Queen's Quay West, Toronto, Ontario, Canada M5J 2N5
Phone 800-463-9951. Internet - www.nauticalmind.com. Select "Search".

Skipper Bob books are also available in e-Book format for all platforms except Kindle. For details go to www.waterwayguide.com and click on "Waterway Guide Store".

Table of Contents

COVID-19 CAUTION

The COVID virus was still very active when this revision was written in January 2021. The operating status of the marinas, restaurants and other retail operations listed may be temporarily or permanently closed after publication.

Chapter 1

The New York Canal System

The New York Canal System today consists of the Erie, Oswego, Cayuga-Seneca, and Champlain Canals. It provides boaters not only with access to some wonderful cruising areas, but is in itself a great place to cruise. During the summer, the warm days and cool nights make boating a real pleasure. Add to that the many quaint and picturesque towns and villages with warm and friendly people and you can understand why so many boaters choose to cruise this area.

A better understanding of the history of the canals in New York will make your cruising both more enjoyable and educational. Canals first began to be used as transportation in the United States at the end of the 1700s. To begin with, a number of small canals were built to transport goods over a short distance. The Dismal Swamp Canal was opened in 1784 for travel between Norfolk, VA and Elizabeth City, NC. A short canal was completed in 1785 near New Orleans called the Carondelet Canal providing a route east to the coastal route to Florida. In 1795 the South Hadley Canal, a 2-½ mile canal, was constructed around a dam on the Connecticut River in Massachusetts. Other canals included the 7-mile canal near Richmond, VA (1789), the 1 mile Conewago Canal on the lower Susquehanna River in Pennsylvania (1797), and the Patowmack Canal on the Potomac in Virginia (1802), just to mention a few.

The first canal (1) of the New York Canal System was the Champlain Canal started in 1817 and completed in 1822, three years ahead of the Erie Canal. This canal connected Waterford, NY, at the junction of the Mohawk and Hudson Rivers, with Whitehall, NY, on Lake Champlain, 60 miles to the north. This provided access to Lake Champlain and Canada via the Richelieu River and Chambly Canal.

In the early 1800s, men of vision began planning a canal from the tidal Hudson River to Buffalo, NY on Lake Erie. This canal, if completed, would dramatically shorten the time necessary to get goods from the East Coast to the Great Lakes and the interior of the United States. At that time, goods had to go over land at great expense from the Hudson River to the Great Lakes. The other option was the long way around up the East Coast and up the Saint Lawrence River to Lake Ontario. Then the falls at the Niagara River had to be overcome via portage of all materials. A canal such as that proposed would greatly reduce the cost of shipping goods to the Midwest.

After much effort, the Erie Canal was started in 1817 and opened to traffic in 1825. A great deal of credit for building the canal must go to Governor DeWitt Clinton, as he spearheaded the effort to build the canal and took much abuse from his opponents during its construction. The project was often referred to as "Clinton's Ditch". However, soon after it opened, the Erie Canal was such a success, that everyone jumped on the bandwagon to support the canal.

The Erie Canal (2) was over 340 miles long and it is the most famous and best known of all the New York Canals. The Erie Canal connected Troy, NY on the Hudson River with Buffalo, NY on Lake Erie. Numerous other canals were constructed to tie into the Erie Canal to form the NY Canal System, which in 1900 was the envy of the world. The Erie Canal has been enlarged and modified over the years, and is still the mainstay of the New York Canal System to this day.

By 1900 New York had many canals. As the picture below shows, you could get your goods to the Erie Canal, and thus the world, from any major location in New York State.

(1) Champlain
(2) Erie
(3) Oswego
(4) Chenango
(5) Genesee
(6) Seneca
(7) Crooked Lake
(8) Dansville Branch
(9) Chemung
(10) Delaware & Hudson
(11) Cayuga
(12) Black River

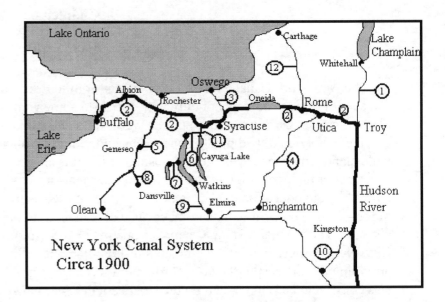

New York Canal System
Circa 1900

The Oswego Canal (3) connected the Erie Canal at Syracuse with Oswego on Lake Ontario. Started in 1819 and completed in 1829, this important branch of the Erie Canal was 38 miles long at that time. The Oswego Canal is still in use, although shortened now, and part of the New York Canal System.

The Cayuga Seneca Canal (11) was completed in 1828 and connected the Erie Canal with Cayuga and Seneca Lakes (two of the Finger Lakes). Only 21 miles long, it was nonetheless important since it opened the Finger Lakes to the Erie Canal. The Cayuga-Seneca Canal is still part of the New York Canal System.

More canals were opened; the Genesee Valley Canal (5) connected Rochester with the Erie Canal and Olean, NY some 80 miles away. The Chenango Canal (4) connected Utica, on the Erie Canal, with Binghamton, NY, near the Pennsylvania border. Other canals were developed as shown in the picture above.

This marvelous transportation system prospered and was very successful. Then in the early 1900s railroads began to develop and provide inexpensive competition to the canals. Soon after, the amount of tonnage shipped via the New York Canal System began to decrease and the canals began to fall into disrepair. One after another the smaller feeder canals were abandoned, until today; all that is left are the Erie, Oswego, Cayuga-Seneca and Champlain Canals. However, these canals in themselves provide over 400 miles of marvelous cruising and provide important links for boaters trying to get to or from the Great Lakes.

Most boaters using the New York Canal System travel between Troy, NY on the Hudson River and Oswego, on Lake Ontario. This trip entails traveling on the Erie Canal some 160 miles roughly east or west and then north or south some 24 miles to Lake Ontario via the Oswego Canal. Still others go from Troy, NY to Buffalo, NY on Lake Erie traversing the entire 341 miles of the Erie Canal. A small percentage of boaters travel north from Troy, NY via the Champlain Canal some 60 miles to visit Lake Champlain each summer. Finally, there are other boaters that just spend the summer traveling around the New York Canal System enjoying one of North America's best cruising areas.

Before you go, you should know -

The balance of this book is divided into sections, one for each of the canals that make up the present day New York Canal System. They are the Erie, Champlain, Cayuga-Seneca and Oswego Canals.

If you are planning a trip to this area, make certain you have the proper charts; paper, electronic, or both. When reviewing the charts, you will find that only part of the Erie Canal has been charted; no charts exist for the western portion from Lyons to Tonawanda.

- **NOAA Chart 14786,** Small Craft Chart Book (61 charts)

If your travel plans include the western half of the Erie Canal, the New York Canal Corporation has published a book of maps of the entire system, including the western end of the Erie Canal. Although the book does not contain charts, with all their nautical detail, the maps are quite good and can be used for the entire New York Canal System. In addition, some information on marinas and other locations along the waterway is included. The book, titled Cruising Guide to the New York State Canal System, is available at many nautical bookstores and online at Landfall Navigation. The cost is $29.95.

Take some time and explore the canals website. It contains a wealth of information (including water depths, bridge clearances, and navigation notices) that will make your journey on the waterway much more pleasant.

Finally, if you enjoy reading, a good source for books on the Erie Canal is the Erie Canal Museum, The Weigh Lock Building, 318 Erie Blvd East, Syracuse, NY 13202, Ph 315-471-0593, or on the Internet at www.eriecanalmuseum.org.

Canal Fees/Controlling Heights/Other Facts

Fees for the 2021 navigation season have been waived. Hours of operation for the entire canal system will be from mid-May to mid-October. Details will be found in Appendix I. Visit nycanals.gov for the most recent information. You may tie up at no charge at most locks, town terminals and docks. Many of these places provide free water and electric hook ups. Details will be found in each of the four canal sections that follow.

Canal water restrictions are few. The controlling depth as posted on the NY Canals website is 14' for the Eastern Erie and Oswego Canals, and 12' for the Western Erie, Cayuga-Seneca and Champlain Canals. Bridge height restrictions are another matter. The Erie Canal from Troy, NY to the Oswego Canal has a controlled height of 21'. The Oswego Canal also has a controlled height of 21'. The Champlain Canal has a controlled height of 17'. (**Note-** be sure to read the note at the beginning of the Chaplain Canal for a detailed explanation of the 17' controlling height for this canal.) The western half of the Erie Canal beyond the Oswego Canal has a controlled height of 15.6'. Finally, the controlled height of the Cayuga-Seneca Canal is 17.5'. All of these clearances are at **normal pool** and may change due to heavy rains or lack thereof. Since none of the bridges have clearance gauges, it is always best to proceed slowly and check your clearance if you are close to the authorized clearance on any stretch of the canals. Normal pool elevations and other data may be found on the NY Canals website. **Note:** The bridge clearances listed in the text is the charted clearance on the NOAA charts and is at **normal pool**.

Check the canal system website (http://www.nyscanals.gov) and click on **Notice to Mariners** to view the latest alerts relative to the waterway. You can also sign up to receive these alerts via email. Another source is www.waterwayguide.com, which is updated daily.

Fuel on the canals is competitively priced and not hard to find. Diesel fuel is not available at all fuel docks but this does not present a problem if you monitor your fuel supply and plan accordingly. To aid in your planning, marinas along the canal system with fuel service and transient dockage are listed at the appropriate mile marker with an indication of the type of fuel they carry, diesel (D), gas (G) and (P) if they offer pump out.

The canal system has an excellent buoy system and navigation is normally a matter of carefully following the charts and watching for shoaling areas, if any. An excellent source to view navigation alerts is www.waterwayguide.com.

Most vessels are held in groups as they lock through the canal system. Thus, when a fast boat locks through with slower boats, speeding up to get to the next lock quickly may very well be a waste of time. Often the faster boats are held in the next lock until the slower vessels catch up and enter the lock.

Unwritten lock etiquette has the first boat take a spot on either wall. As other boats enter the locks, they alternate sides tying up close to the vessel ahead of them. When leaving, boats exit in the same sequence as when they entered the lock. This assures the maximum number of vessels in each locking and the easiest maneuvering within the lock.

The entire canal system is designated a no-discharge zone. All vessels are banned from discharging sewage, even treated sewage from Lectra-San type units, into the canals.

Mail, Email, Cell Phone & Internet

If you spend some time on the New York Canal System, you may want to receive mail, even in today's digital age and all it encompasses. The easiest way is to have it forwarded in a single package via Priority Mail to the Post Office, General Delivery, in a town near the canal. Have your mail forwarded to the following address: Your name, General Delivery, Town, State, Zip Code. The post office will hold your mail for 10 days before returning the package. Not all post offices hold mail, so call to determine the availability of this service. Cell phone coverage is generally good throughout the system. Internet service is also adequate, and several stops offer WiFi.

Canadian Competency Requirements

If your travel on The New York Canals is eventually going to take you into Canadian waters, Canadian regulations require that all operators of pleasure craft fitted with a motor have a proof of competency and proof of age on board at all times. This applies to *non-residents* who operate their craft in Canadian waters for more than 45 consecutive days, or operate a vessel that is registered or licensed in Canada, including rentals. For complete details visit the Transport Canada website (www.tc.gc.ca) and at the bottom of the home page click on Boating Safety. Then select "paperwork".

Locking Through

When you enter any of the locks, your first concern is how to secure your vessel while you lock up or down. There are three basic types of locks. One type has several pipes running down both sides of the lock. This is the easiest type of lock to traverse. Simply pull up to one of these pipes amidships and run a line around the pipe. Next secure one end of the rope to a cleat amidships. Finally, loosely loop the bitter end of the line around the same cleat, but stand by the line so you can release it in an

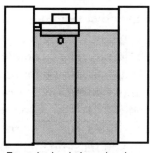
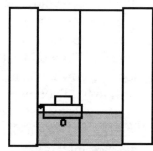

Boat in lock in raised position.

Boat in lock in lowered position.

emergency. Now, as your vessels rises or drops, the line slides up or down the pipe and holds your vessel in place. Three large fenders evenly spaced along the side of your vessel keep it off the lock walls and slide up or down easily on the wet slimy walls. Watch for large holes in lock walls. Push your vessel off to allow the fenders to clear these holes and not get swallowed up in them. Also, watch your freeboard. The pipe stops just below the top of the lock wall. If the lock is filling and your vessel has a lot of freeboard, you may rise above the end of the pipe. In this case, you will need to let out some line from the amidships cleat as your vessel rises above the edge of the lock.

The second type of lock has sets of steel cables anchored top and bottom in several places along both sides of the lock walls. These cables are

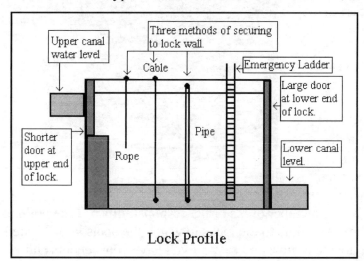

Lock Profile

coated with rubber to avoid damaging your line. Use the same procedure as with the steel pipes and come alongside one of these cables amidships. Secure a line around the cable to your amidships cleat and ride the cable up or down the lock wall.

The third and least desirable type of lock simply has ropes hanging down the lock wall in several places on both sides of the lock. Unfortunately, this is one of the most common types of lock you will encounter on the New York Canal System. In this case you bring your vessel in between two of these ropes. One member of your crew takes the forward rope and one holds the aft rope. You will want a pair of old gloves for this type of lock. The ropes are wet, dirty, and slimy. Do not pull too tightly on the lines to try to hold your vessel against the lock walls. If you do, the person on the bow ends up fighting the person on the stern as you alternately pull the bow and stern in against the lock wall.

For your convenience, next to the lock name and mileage location in the navigation section, the method for securing is listed; pipes (P), cables (C), ropes (R). In some instances more than one method may be shown.

The first lock can be intimidating! When locking up, as the water first enters the lock, it creates a wave and you may swing a fair amount. As the lock fills however, the swinging action greatly subsides and you can enjoy the lift. When locking down, there is virtually no swinging motion of the boat, and it is a very smooth ride. On the other side of the coin, it is easier to get a line secured to your vessel when locking up since the pole/cable/rope is right in front of you, and you simply have to reach out for it. When locking down, the pole/cable/rope is down near your waterline and can be difficult to reach. When locking down, you may want to throw a temporary line around a bollard or ladder handrail on the lock wall to hold you in place until your vessel is lowered below the top of the lock wall. Then you can easily secure your vessel to the pole/cable/rope as previously described.

Generally you can tie up either port or starboard, as you prefer, when in the locks. However, there are a couple of locks where you must tie up on only one side of the lock, because of the way the water enters the lock. The helpful lock crews will usually tell you about this problem before you get to the lock. In addition, since a lot of maintenance is being performed on these locks, you may be asked to tie to one side or another, because of work crews. But, in general, you can lock through on whichever side you prefer.

Locks and lift bridges are contacted on VHF channel 13 and you will find the lock staff to be cheerful, helpful, and understanding. Feel free to ask them for the best places to stay and where to get supplies or to eat. Also, be sure to tell each crew how much further you plan to go. That way, they can call ahead and have the next lock/bridge waiting for you.

Do not plan on the lock crew assisting you in locking your boat. They are busy with other duties. However, do not hesitate to ask them about anything you might be uncertain about regarding locking procedures or information about the local surroundings. You will find they are pleasant and want your trip to be a good one.

On occasion a vessel will enter a lock and have trouble getting secured. You do not want to be near a vessel that is having a difficult time. Remain calm in the lock. Yelling and screaming at each other does not help the situation. Know what your

Inside Lock 3

duties are while in the lock and brief each crewmember of his or her responsibilities. Take nothing for granted. Expect to put on a show. Many tourists come to the locks to watch the boats lock through. Expect a crowd to be watching. The best advice is slow and easy. If you have your fenders and lines ready before you get to the lock, you are ahead of the game. Have your crew get out their gloves and poles before you enter the lock. Advise the whole crew which side of the lock you will tie up on and which pole/cable/set of ropes you plan to use as soon as you can determine them.

The New York Canal System locks do not operate 24 hours a day, as do many of the locks operated by the Corps of Engineers throughout the interior United States. Rather they generally operate from 8 AM to 6:00 PM between mid- May through early September. During early May and during the fall hours are 7 AM to 5 PM. Appendix 1 lists the hours of operation or you can check the canal system website for current operating hours. (Note: At press time the hours of operation for 2021 had not been established).

Speed limits are, except where posted, unlimited on the lakes, 45 mph on the rivers, 10 mph in land and rock cuts, and 5 mph within 100 feet of a dock, pier, raft or mooring float.

Overnight Options

In addition to the numerous marinas along the canals, complimentary tie-up space can generally be found at most locks and towns along the way. You should be aware that terminals owned and operated by the Canal Corporation have a maximum stay of 48 hours. (See Chapter 3, Waterford for details) Towns along the canal have renovated terminal walls and provide complimentary dockage or charge a very low rate. Many of these facilities have electric, water and other amenities. These facilities and their amenities are listed at the appropriate mile marker in this guide.

Mileage Calculation

In the chapter on each of the four canals is a list of canal highlights pertaining to that section on the New York Canal System. Each of the four canals covered in this publication has been marked off in statute miles from the canals point of origin to the end. All canal highlights are referenced to these mile markers. Since your chart/map book will not have these mile markers, the town name, lock number, bridge number, etc. is also listed. You might want to consider marking the mileages on your charts.

Mile markers are especially helpful when you are trying to judge how far you need to go in a day and/or how long it will take you to get to a particular point. To calculate how far you can go in a day, simply figure out how many miles you can go at your normal cruising speed (must be 10 MPH or less on New York Canal System). Now look at how many locks you must traverse in that distance. Deduct 30 minutes of travel for each lock and either reduce your target distance by that amount, or increase your estimate travel time by 30 minutes per lock.

Here is an example of how that works. You are tied up at Lock 11 (mile 38.8) for the night. You normally make 7 MPH when cruising. You don't like to travel more than 6 hours in a day. How far will you go the next day barring bad weather or unforeseen delays? Normally you would go 42 miles in a day (7 x 6). You add 42 to your present mileage of 38.8 and find you would end up at mile 80.8. A quick check of the Erie Canal Highlights shows that mile 80.8 would put you between Lock 17 and 18. To get that far, you would have to traverse 6 locks (locks 12 through 17). You must either add 3 hours (30 minutes per lock) to your cruising time (6 + 3 = 9) or reduce your estimated distance you want to travel so that you go through fewer locks. If you want to travel closer to 6 hours, suppose you target west of lock 15 for that day, instead of 42 miles. Lock 15 is at mile 64.3 and only 25.5 miles travel and four locks (12 through 15). The 25.5 miles would require 3.6 plus hours and the four locks would require an additional 2 hours for 5.6 plus hours travel time. Closer to your desired 6 hours travel per day.

Interpreting the Book

To add to your ease of traveling on the New York Canal System, all locks and lift bridges are listed whether they provide a place to stop or not. Further, the distance raised or lowered in feet is listed in parenthesis behind each lock number. As an example; "**Lock 14**(8') (R)". Lock 14 provides a lift of 8 feet. As indicated earlier, the second letter in brackets indicates whether the lock has ropes (R), pipes (P) or cables (C). The term "**15A electric**" refers to a standard household receptacle. Often these are on 20A breakers. "**30A or 50A electric**" refers to standard marine plugs. The term "**short wall**" refers to a wall where only one or two boats could normally tie up. Directions such as "**north, south, east** or **west**" may not refer to true compass directions. Rather, they assume the canal runs east or west (such as the Erie Canal) or north and south (such as the Champlain Canal) and give a direction away from the Canal or in reference to the direction the canal runs.

Fenders

Three large fenders for each side are adequate for a vessel in the 45-foot range. Consider a minimum of 10" x 30" for cylinders. Another option is to use round fenders. Do not skimp on fender protection. The lock walls and some of the terminal walls are rough and can do a lot of damage to gelcoat.

Fenders will get dirty, however, if they are cleaned thoroughly at the end of the trip it is no problem. Some boaters cover their fenders with burlap or some other cloth and then discard it at the end of the trip.

Still other boaters swear by fender boards. Although fender boards work well against pilings, they do not slide up and down the lock walls very well.

Stepping Your Mast

Sailboats can get their masts stepped or un-stepped at marinas on all ends of the canals. On the Hudson River you can stop at Riverview Marine Services (518-943-5311) or Hop-O-Nose Marina (518-943-4640), both on the Catskill River about 41 miles south of Troy. Or you can stop at the Castleton Boat Club (518-732-7077), 16.6 miles south of Troy and "do-it-yourself" by paying a fee to use their crane.

At the west end of the Erie Canal in North Tonawanda, NY you can use the services of the Wardell Boatyard (716-692-9428) located on the north side of the canal just before the first fixed bridge when east bound on the canal. Or you can use the services of Rich Marine Sales (716-873-4060) or RCR Yachts (716-856-6314) in Buffalo. On the Oswego Canal southbound, mast stepping is done at the Oswego Marina (315-342-0436), just north of the entrance to the Oswego Canal on the east side. Finally, on the north end of the Champlain Canal, masts can be stepped at Chipman Point Marina (802) 558-4574 in Ordell, VT.

Each of the marinas steps, or un-steps, masts for a fee. It is best to call ahead and make reservations. If un-stepping your mast, the lumber for mast cradles to support the mast on your deck can usually be found at these marinas in the form of used cradles of boats which stepped their masts there. For unusually long masts, be sure and check to see if the marina can handle a mast that size. In some cases, very large masts will have to be stepped or un-stepped at a shipyard some distance from the canals.

Summary

Warning! The information given in this book should not be used for navigation. The material provided is designed to aid you in enjoying your cruise on the New York Canal System, not to aid you in navigation. Navigation must be performed based on NOAA charts using proper navigation tools.

Conditions that change all the time such as water depth, bridge height restrictions, submerged vessels, and location of day markers are not included in this publication. You should use the approved Notice to Mariners for this information, the New York Canals Corporation website, or the Waterway Guide website. **Do not use the material in this book for navigation.**

Contributors

Your comments/updates are encouraged and welcomed. Email tstehle@waterwayguide.com.

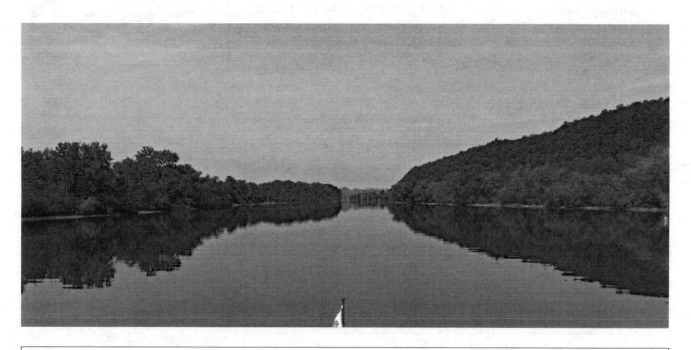

Mohawk River
Photo Courtesy of Glen and Jill Moore
m/v Last Dance

Chapter 2

The Erie Canal

The Erie Canal was a real engineering marvel in its day. Originally 363 miles long, it connected the Hudson River with Lake Erie and the other Great Lakes and opened the entire

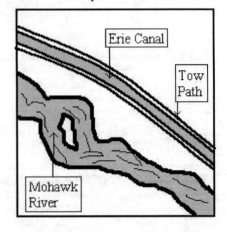

population in the center of this country to shipping to and from the rest of the world. Construction of the canal began in 1817 and finished in 1825. The original Erie Canal was very different from the Erie Canal you will boat on today. It was designed as a ditch filled with water. Mules or horses could walk beside the ditch on a towpath and pull the boats through. For this reason, the original canal followed the river's course to take advantage of the fairly level terrain, but did not use the riverbed as part of the canal. In fact, the canal was normally a ditch dug alongside the river. When it came time to cross a river or creek, it was necessary to build an aqueduct across the river or creek to carry the canal water and the path for the horses and mules.

The original canal was only 4 feet deep and 40 feet wide and designed to carry small canal boats with loads of 30 tons. The canal was a huge success, and boat traffic increased

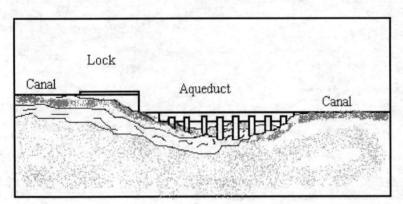

The canal used locks to change elevation as the river headed downstream. When it was necessary to cross a river, the canal used an aqueduct. But, as always, the water in the canal was nearly level.

dramatically. Soon the canal was deepened and its course altered as necessary, and by 1862 was 7 feet deep and could carry boats of 240 tons. At the turn of the century the canal was once again enlarged to carry more and larger vessels. More importantly, now many of the vessels were self-propelled and the canal could follow natural waterways and lakes.

By 1903, when the present day Erie Canal was completed, it was not located where the original canal had been. Although their paths cross, the present day Erie Canal follows the natural rivers and lakes to a much greater degree than the original Erie Canal. However, you can still see some of the original smaller locks and stretches of the Erie Canal that have been preserved.

Today the Erie Canal has a minimum depth of 12 feet from Troy to Buffalo. It traverses 35 locks (34 on the Erie Canal and the Federal Lock at Troy), as it rises, then falls and finally rises from sea level at Troy to 565 feet above sea level at the Niagara River. Over 200 highway and railroad bridges cross the canal with a controlled height of 20 feet from Troy to the Oswego

Canal and 15 ½ feet from the Oswego Canal to the Niagara River. The locks are numbered 2 through 35. There is no lock 1 or 31 on the Erie Canal. However, there are two locks 28, A and B. As lock numbers changed or locks were eliminated, the rest of the locks were not renumbered. It would be too costly. Missing lock numbers is not unusual. The Oswego Canal has no lock 4 and the Champlain Canal has no lock 10.

For many, cruising the Erie Canal is an adventure. They proceed slowly, stop often and stay several days at many different locations. They stay at marinas, tie to lock walls, and utilize the many town docks. Many towns along the canals have festivals and other events that are a joy to attend, and there certainly is a lot of history to review.

Comparing the Canals		
The Original Erie or Grand	Enlarged 1862 Canal	Present Day Erie Canal
363 miles long	350.5 miles	340.7 miles
Canal 40' x 4'	Canal 70' x 7'	Canal 123' x 12'
83 Locks	72 Locks	34 Locks
15'x90'x4'	18'x110'x7'	44.5'x300'x12'
Clearance=	11 feet	15 ½ feet

The trip across the Erie Canal begins in Troy, NY. You proceed a short distance north of Troy on the Hudson River to the Troy Federal Lock (Open 6AM to 10PM). This is the only lock operated by the Corps of Engineers. The New York State Canal Corporation, which is a part of the New York Power Authority, operates all the rest. After proceeding north from the Troy Lock 2.3 statute miles you come to the junction of the Mohawk and Hudson Rivers at Waterford, NY. Just north of red marker "242" you proceed to port past Green "1" and enter the Erie Canal. Waterford, which is on the north shore, has been designated one of the seven "waterfront centers" in the Canal Recreation Plan. At the Waterford Harbor Visitor Center you will find a 1,000 foot floating dock and a 600 foot concrete wall for tie up, with complimentary water, bathrooms, showers, shore power, pump out and WiFi service. You may tie up here for two nights, free. This is an excellent location to make final preparations to your vessel. Make certain your air draft is low enough and secure your fenders on each side. It is also a good idea to walk the short distance up to Lock 2 and purchase your canal pass. This way, you won't hold everyone up in the morning when you start west, because you won't have to buy your pass after you get in the lock. While at lock 2 look at the historical display and the old locks. Also, if you did not order the Northern Cartographic Cruising Guide to the New York Canal System, you can get it at the Waterford Visitor Center.

Please note, that had you not turned to port at this point, but proceeded on north up the Hudson River, you would have entered the Champlain Canal and been on your way to Lake Champlain. The Champlain Canal is covered in Chapter 7 of this book.

When you leave the terminal wall at Waterford headed west, you first encounter a series of five locks, known as the Waterford Flight, which will raise your boat 169 feet in elevation in less than two miles. You are not permitted to stop overnight between these locks, so you must allow yourself enough time to get through all five before you want to stop for the day. Plan on about two hours to complete these first five locks, numbers 2 to 6. The first lock on the Erie Canal system going west is numbered as Lock 2. This occurred because the Troy Lock was originally considered Lock 1. However, since it is now a Federal lock and not part of the Erie Canal or New York Canal System, it is not considered part of the Erie Canal today. Thus, the Erie Canal consists of locks 2 through 35. (No lock 1 or 31)

The Erie Canal can best be described if it is divided up into the Eastern, Middle and Western Sections.

Eastern Section of the Erie Canal

On the Eastern Section, the first five locks raise you above the Hudson River escarpment and you follow the Mohawk River west. Most of the time, you travel in the Mohawk River bed and the waterway is fairly wide with buoys and cans marking the sides of the channel. The Eastern Section of the Erie Canal follows the natural waterway, as does the Interstate Highway and railroads. Because of this, you frequently see and hear both the road and train traffic. While you pass through Schenectady and Scotia, the canal does not provide good access to either of these large cities and you would probably not even know when you went by them, were it not for the charts.

This is not to imply that there are no places to stop. On the contrary, there are many nice little towns and villages along the way, where you can stop and explore or shop. These include Amsterdam, Canajoharie, Ft. Plain, Little Falls, Herkimer and Utica.

Past Herkimer, the Erie Canal leaves the Mohawk River and becomes a true canal running alongside the narrow winding river as the canal approaches the high point of the Eastern section; Rome, NY. In the early 1800s, Rome, NY was the portage point for canoes and small boats coming up the Mohawk River and heading west. It was here that boats were removed from the Mohawk River and carried across land to Wood Creek to continue their journey west via Lake Oneida to Lake Ontario. Because of this, a fort was built at Rome and this fort provided control of this important river route. Today, Fort Stanwix has been completely restored and is located about 8 blocks from the terminal in Rome. It is well worth the stop to visit and learn.

The Middle Section of the Erie Canal

The middle section of the Erie Canal starts at Rome, NY. From this point west, the canal first drops in elevation as it approaches the level of the Oswego River. Then the Erie Canal rises in elevation, as it follows the Seneca River west and slowly rises to the elevation of the Cayuga-Seneca Canal and continues to rise via locks to Lyons, NY.

The middle section contains so much, you could easily spend a month here. The first major stop you come to, as you go west from Rome, is Sylvan Beach on the east end of Lake Oneida. Sylvan Beach is a neat little summer beach town. The population swells during the summer and there is an amusement park, many restaurants, and a nice long wall to tie to. After a pleasant stop in Sylvan Beach, you cross Lake Oneida. This is the largest body of water on the Erie Canal, 20 miles long and 3 mile wide, and shallow. It should be crossed only after careful consideration of the weather as it can be very rough in the prevailing westerly winds. It is also frequently fog bound and course-plotting prior to crossing is required.

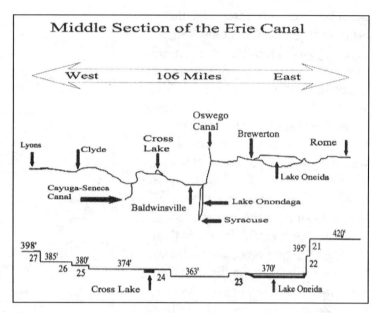

From Lake Oneida, you proceed to the Junction of the Seneca and Oneida Rivers, which becomes the Oswego River (Three Rivers Point). If you are traveling north to Lake Ontario, this is where you leave the Erie Canal. The trip up the Oswego Canal is covered in Section 5 of this book. The Oswego Canal is the low point in elevation of the Erie Canal in the Middle Section. From here on west, the canal steadily rises in elevation via locks as it approaches Lake Erie.

As you follow the Erie Canal west, the next point of interest is Onondaga Lake. Proceed south into this lake and stop at the marina in Liverpool. You can tie up there during the day at no charge while you visit the Salt Museum in Liverpool. The old port of Syracuse has been completely renovated and provides a great stop with a short walk to a large mall. However, the water getting into the old port of Syracuse is very shallow, only 5'. In addition there is a low 17' fixed RR bridge right at the entrance to the port.

Proceeding west through the middle section of the Erie Canal, you can stop at Baldwinsville, spend time on Cross Lake, and finally come to the junction of the Cayuga-Seneca Canal. The Cayuga-Seneca Canal is covered in Section 6 of this book and if time permits is a must side trip off the Erie Canal.

Past the Cayuga-Seneca Canal you approach the end of the Middle Section at Lyons, NY. At mile 208 you come to Lock 26. Just past the topside of this lock is a fixed railroad bridge, E-93. It has a charted vertical clearance of 16'. Even though there is no tide effect in the canal, water levels do change as a result of rain or the lack of it. Make certain you have checked the depth of the canal and that you can clear this bridge.

The Western Section of the Erie Canal

From Lyons west you enter the Western Section of the Erie Canal and leave your charts behind. If you obtained the previously recommended, "Cruising Guide to the New York Canal System by Northern Cartographic", at least you will have a map to follow. This section of the canal more closely resembles the original Erie Canal than any other. From Lyons to Buffalo you continue to lock up as you approach the Niagara River and 565 feet in elevation. The Western Section does not have many locks, but does have 15 lift bridges. Long straight sections, a narrow waterway, many picturesque towns, and a whole plethora of places to stop mark this section. Further, many of the places to stop on this section have free water and/or electric; far more than either of the two preceding sections.

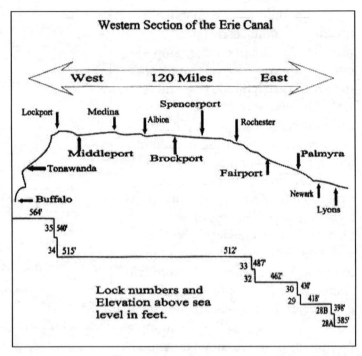

The lift bridges on the Erie Canal are different from those on the Intracoastal Waterway. They offer a clearance of about 17 feet when open. Roving operators operate most of the bridges. Thus, when you go through one bridge, you may have to wait until the operator can get to the second or third bridge. They also operate on VHF channel 13, so keep them informed of how far you plan to go. This way, you will experience a minimum of delay.

There are many great places to stop on the Western Section; Fairport, Spencerport, Brockport, Medina, and Lockport, just to mention a few.

Lockport is near the end of the Western Section of the Erie Canal and has the last two locks on the Erie Canal. Next to the two "new" locks are 5 of the "old" original locks, plus a canal museum.

Finally, you come to Tonawanda. Just a mile west, the Erie Canal enters the Niagara River. Unless you plan to cross or cruise on Lake Erie, there is no point in going beyond Tonawanda. Tonawanda offers excellent shopping, good public transportation, and a fine place for cruisers to stop.

Why Visit the Erie Canal?

A cruiser could easily spend the entire summer on the Erie Canal, moving every few days. There are many wonderful towns and locks at which to stop and visit. Many provide electricity; some have water and pump outs. Most stops are free except for those listed in the highlighted section of the Erie Canal as having a small fee. If the history of the Erie Canal fascinates you, there is much to see. Starting at Lock 2, where 3 of the old locks are preserved, you can visit mini museums and learn a lot about the canal's history. At Rome, visit the Erie Canal Village by taxi. Here you will find a canal village, circa 1840, with most of its original buildings and a canal museum. As you come in to Medina, the present Erie Canal crosses the Orchard Creek on an aqueduct. Thus, you get to take your boat across an aqueduct, something most boaters never get to do. And certainly not last, visit the Erie Canal Museum at Lockport and see 5 of the original locks side by side with 2 of the present day locks.

Do Not Use for Navigation

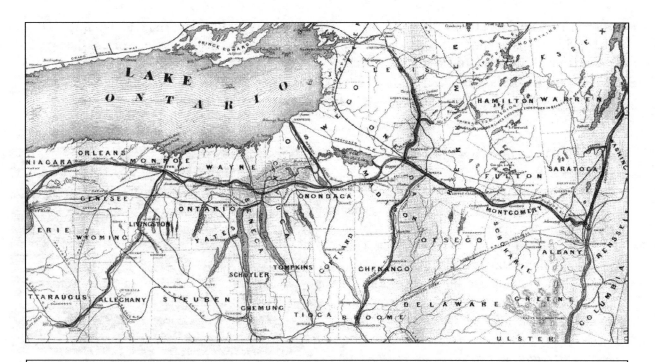

Old Erie Canal map, circa 1850, showing the canal going south of Lake Oneida. The Oswego Canal had to be 14 miles longer to reach the original Erie Canal near Syracuse, NY. Today the Erie Canal passes well to the north of Syracuse, going through Lake Oneida.

Chapter 3

The Eastern Erie Canal

The Erie Canal junction with the Hudson River is just above Peebles Island and marker G1. The fixed bridge spanning the canal at mile 0.41 has a charted vertical clearance of 26'. Just past this bridge is the Waterford Harbor.

This chapter deals with the canal from Waterford, NY west to the junction of the Erie Canal and the Oswego Canal, often referred to as "Three Rivers". All comments are in mile marker sequence.

Mile 0.47, **Waterford**, **Free Dock.** As you leave the Hudson River, the fixed bridge spanning the river at Waterford (E-1 on the chart) has a charted vertical clearance of 27'. Tie up at the Waterford Harbor Visitor Center. The maximum stay is limited by NY law. The following is a summary of the regulation taken from the NY Canals website: *Under the New York Codes, Rules & Regulations, vessels may moor at a Canal Corporation owned dock or terminal up to 48 hours in a calendar month. Such mooring is free of charge,*

Waterford Harbor Visitors Center

though services provided at the facility, such as electric, water and pump outs, may have a charge associated with them. Vessels wishing to moor in excess of 48 hours must apply for a permit from the Corporation. Unless extenuating circumstances exist, such permits are usually granted only to commercial and other non-recreational vessels.

West of the bridge there is a 1000' floating dock. East of the bridge is a 600' concrete wall. **Note:** Do not tie up at the red line on the floating dock, as this marks the pump out station. The floating dock has 30/50A electric ($10/stay), water, showers ($10 deposit) and WiFi. (The concrete wall does not have electric or water. A few 15A residential outlets are located on the sewage pump house.) The coin operated pump out at the floating dock is $3.50. Bring your own adapter.

This stop is always crowded and as a result, you may not be able to tie to the floating docks and thus will use the concrete wall.

Restaurants, a post office and a pizzeria are located within six blocks. A laundry is 4 blocks away. Walk ¼ mile west along the canal to the mini museum at Lock 2. For groceries and other shopping, walk 3 blocks north to Route 4 and turn east. Cross the Hudson River to shop at Price Choppers Supermarket, Burger King, Hannaford Food Store, Rite Aid pharmacy and a liquor store. Hannaford Food will permit you to take a shopping cart back to the Waterford Visitor Center but you must return it. During the season a farmer's market is held on the pier every Sunday morning.

Waterford celebrates Canal Fest in early May, the start of the New York Canal Cruise in early July, and the Tug Boat Round-up on the weekend after Labor Day. During events when the harbor is closed to transient boats the canal corporation allows docking above Lock E3.

Note: You must arrive at a lock at least 20 minutes prior to the scheduled closing time for the day. At the Waterford Flight (Locks E-4, 5, 6), you must arrive at least 90 minutes prior to scheduled closing time, as it takes 90 minutes to transient the flight and there is no overnight docking within the flight.

Mile 0.57, **Bridge E-2, Fourth St** (25.37')

Mile 0.63, **Lock E2, Waterford** (34') **(R**). Vessels are not allowed to tie up between Lock E2 and Guard Gate 2 (mile 2.77).

Historical Note. Be sure to take the time to look at the 3 old locks located next to the newer lock. These locks are now used as overflow for water in the canal. There is also a nice historical display of the park at lock 2. The original Champlain Canal crossed 200' to the west of lock 2 and the remains of this waterway can be seen today. There are two nice walking trails. The north trail leads to an old weigh lock and then to Old Champlain Canal Lock 5, a distance of about 2 miles. The south trail leads to Old Champlain Canal Lock 4, also about 2 miles. Both locks date to the Civil War era.

Mile 0.84, **Bridge E-3, Saratoga Ave** (21.78')

Mile 0.97 **Bridge E-4, railroad** (21.75')

Mile 1.09, **Lock E3, Waterford** (35') (R). When Waterford is crowded due to harbor events, it is possible to overnight on the pier above Lock E3. Contact 518-461-0942 to tie up at this remote location. Note the enormous dry dock alongside.

Mile 1.60, **Lock E4, Waterford** (35') (R&C).

Mile 1.87, **Lock E5, Waterford** (33') (R&C).

Mile 2.15, **Lock E6, Crescent** (33') (R).

Mile 2.52, **Guard Gate 1, Crescent** (24.10'). Normally open.

Mile 2.77, **Guard Gate 2, Crescent** (24.10'). The only guard gate normally closed. You may have to call on VHF channel 13 or 518-237-0833 to get it opened. West of Guard Gate 2, **Free Dock.** Tie up on the south wall adjacent to a canal park. You can also tie up adjacent to the park on the north side, however, there are houses, a parking lot and boat launch ramp close by. There are no cleats or rings to tie to, only fixed bollards set back from the wall and widely spaced. Long lines required. Can be rough if winds are out of the NW.

Mile 2.78, **Bridge E-5, Guard Gate Rd** (24.30')

Mile 4.32, **Albany Marine Service,** (518-783-5333, G,P) 30/50A electric service. On the south bank, east of bridge E-6.

Mile 4.50, **Village of Crescent, Free Dock.** 200' east of bridge E-6, tie up to north wall. Two fixed bollards. Stewarts convenience store ½ block north. Some road noise.

Mile 4.55, **Bridge E-6, Loudon Rd, State Route 9** (24.19')

Mile 5.96, **Crescent Boat Club,** (518-928-7588, G,P,WiFi) On the north bank at R14.

Mile 6.88, **Blain's Bay Marina,** (518-785-6785, G,P) On the south bank east of bridge E-7A.

Mile 7.10, **Diamond Reef Yacht Club,** (518-235-5748) On the north bank east of bridge E-7A.

Mile 7.21, **Bridge E-7A, Northway, I-87** (30.27').

Mile 13.07, **Lock E7, Vischer Ferry** (27') (R). West of Lock 7, **Free Dock,** tie up on the short south lock wall **behind the wall**. Recommend you exercise caution if using this wall. It is made up of rough steel plates and has a steel beam protruding below the water. Proper placement of fenders is required. This is a quiet rural stop with picnic tables. Adjacent to the site is a bike trail that runs along the canal.

Lock E-7, Vischer Ferry
Photo courtesy Tug44.org

Mile 17.2, **Schenectady Yacht Club,** (518-384-9971, G,D,P) 30/50/100A electrical service, showers. Behind the yacht club is part of the old Erie Canal and one of the 1862 locks. The lock is now used by the Schenectady Yacht Club as a boat haul bay at the end of the old Erie Canal. Known for being very accommodating.

Mile 17.24, **Historical Note:** Just east of bridge E-8, both north and south of the canal are the remains of an early aqueduct which spanned the Mohawk River.

Mile 17.25, **Bridge E-8, Balltown Rd** (25.18')

Mile 17.8, **Caution.** Follow the markers carefully through the submerged remains of the Schenectady-Saratoga Trolley Bridge.

Schenectady Yacht Club
Photo courtesy Tug44.org

Mile 18.14, **Mohawk Valley Marine,** (518-399-2719) On the north bank west of R70.

Mile 19.80, **Bridge E-10, railroad** (26.70')

Mile 20.12, **Bridge E-11**, **Freeman's Bridge** (25.10'),

Mile 20.5, **Mohawk Harbor**, (518-949-0220, WiFi) A
new multi-purpose complex with marina,
restaurants, retail shops, casino, offices and
amphitheater. Currently under development, but
the marina and several estabishments are open.

Mile 20.99, **Bridge E-12, railroad** (24.30')

Mile 21.61, **Bridge E-13, State St**. (27.00')

Mile 21.61, **Scotia Landing**. Just prior to R100 turn to
starboard and follow the unmarked channel
behind Isle of the Cayugas. Slips for 8 vessels at
Freedom Park. Water, 30amp.

The remains of the 1842 Rexford
Aqueduct
Photo courtesy Tug44.org

Mile 23.8, **Isle of the Oneidas.** Just prior to R112 turn to starboard and follow the unmarked
channel. Anchor in 8-10 feet.

Mile 24.04, **Lock E8, Scotia** (14') (R), **Free Dock.** East or west of the lock, tie up on the south
wall. Some turbulence from dam on east end. No power available. Train and highway
noise. Park with picnic tables. Foot bridge clearance 23'.

Mile 25.73, **Bridge E-14A, Interstate 890** (22.37')

Mile 26.06, **Arrowhead Marina and RV Park,** (518-382-8966, P) On north bank west of R134.
Note: Maximum length accommodated is 40 feet.

Mile 27.11, **Bridge E-15, railroad** (24.40')

Mile 29.06. **Caution** – You may experience a strong
current from the adjacent dam. Watch as you
approach Lock E9.

Mile 29.07, **Lock E9, Rotterdam** (15') (R). Rebuilt in
2014. The sunken cement barges that were on
the north bank at the east and west ends of the
lock have been removed.

Mile 29.08, **Bridge E-16, SR 103** (23.19')

Hurricane Irene damage to Lock 10
Photo courtesy Tug44.org

Mile 30.43, **Bridge E-17, railroad** (24.42')

Mile 35.02, **Lock E10, Cranesville** (15') (R), **Free Dock.** East or west of the lock tie up on south wall. You will encounter a lot of train noise. **Note:** This lock and its surroundings suffered extensive damage from Hurricane Irene in August 2011. The foot bridge clearance is 23'.

Mile 37.95, **Amsterdam.** Riverlink Park offers 600' of docking space with 30/50/A electric, water, pump out, laundry, showers, bathrooms and WiFi. Overnight dockage is $1.00/ft. (January 2020). Call on VHF 13 or phone 518-320-4868. Saturday concerts in the summer. River's Edge Café on site. It is a short walk via the overpass (locked at 10pm – elevator and stairs) to some shopping and Professional Wrestlers Hall of Fame. Note on the chart that this dock is adjacent to train tracks.

Riverlink Park in Amsterdam
Photo courtesy Tug44.org

Historical Note. Amsterdam was once home to the Mohawk Carpet Mills. Competition destroyed this once vibrant business and fire finished off the mill buildings. Amsterdam suffered greatly when the weaving business left but has a vibrant revitalization program. One famous past resident of this town is Kirk Douglas, the actor.

Mile 38.06, **Bridge E-19A, State Route 30** (38.29')

Mile 39.29, **Lock E11, Amsterdam** (12') (R), **Free Dock.** Lock walls rough. Tie up to wall east or west of lock on north bank. Next to train tracks, can be noisy. West of the lock is Guy Park. The western end of the park wall has 3 power pedestals, each with one 50A and 30A connector. Approximately 1-mile west is an Amtrak Station, and 2 miles west is Old Fort Johnson and its museum. Russo's Grill is nearby (365 W. Main St.). Stewarts convenience store is also close by.

Guy Park
Photo Courtesy of Glen and Jill Moore
m/v Last Dance

Mile 43.52, **Lock E12, Tribes Hill** (11') (R&P), Free Dock. Tie up to east or west of lock on north lock wall. Rural setting, park, but considerable train noise. Shady and pretty. Approximately a ¾ mile walk to Schoharie Crossing across the bridge, where there are remnants of the original Erie Canal complete with a visitor's center (closed on Tuesday). **Note:** This lock also suffered substantial damage from Hurricane Irene. Repairs were completed in 2015. The bridge has a clearance of 22'.

Mile 43.85, **Historical Note.** On the south shore, Schoharie Creek enters the canal. About ½ mile up the creek are the remains of an original Erie Canal aqueduct, which crossed the creek at this point. Four of the stone arches survive to this date. Water depth in the center of the creek is good for about 0.4 miles (to just before the aqueduct) and it is possible to anchor here, but holding is not good. Do not attempt to pass the aqueduct; the water is shallow and the bottom very rocky. Don't anchor if strong winds or unsettled weather is expected. One-half mile beyond the aqueduct remains the NY Thruway crosses

Schoharie Crossing Aqueduct
Photo courtesy Tug 44.org

Schoharie Creek. This is the area where the bridge collapsed in 1987 taking 5 cars with it.

Mile 48.52, **Bridge E-23, State Route 30A** (23.20')

Mile 48.63, **Fonda, Free Dock.** Tie up at the high terminal wall west of bridge E-23 on the north bank. This is a gated Canal Corp maintenance facility and the gate closes at 3:30pm. Two options when you depart the dock area. First, turn north on Bridge Street South for Dairy bar (0.2 mile) and restaurant. Continue north to Route 5 (0.4 mile) and turn left (west). At 0.7 miles, you will come to a Subway, Chinese Restaurant, Pizzeria, and Stewart's Convenience Store. At 0.8 mile is a Dollar General Store. Finally, there is a laundromat at 0.9 mile.

As your second option, cross bridge to south bank of canal and walk east to McDonalds and restaurants with in ½ mile. Very urban. **Note:** If you get locked in cross under the bridge and walk up the berm to the road.

Historical Note. The Henry Fonda clan is from Fonda, NY.

Mile 53.12, **Lock E13, Randall** (8') (R&P), **Free Dock**. Tie up east or west of lock on south lock wall. East wall is very tall.

Mile 60.55, **Canajoharie Riverfront Park, Free Dock**. Just east of bridge E-24 on the south side are floating docks with 30/50A electric. If the dock is full you can turn south east of the floating docks into terminal basin and tie up on west wall. Water shoals quickly near I-90 Bridge. This wall has no cleats or electric. Bring long lines to tie to widely spaced barge posts. Some train and road noise.

Picturesque River Front Park with picnic tables, and gliders. Easy walk (all within 3 blocks) to PO, restaurants (Mercato's, Tony's, and Village Restaurant), ATM, Village

Apothecary drugstore, convenient stores, gift shops, art gallery and antiques, Peruzzi's Meat Market with groceries. Stewart's convenience store is across the bridge.

Across bridge E-24 to the north side of the canal it's 1 block to McDonalds, Rite Aid Pharmacy, Post Office, and Dollar General. An ACE hardware is 1.5 miles east. Be sure to check out Stewart's for great ice cream.

Canajoharie is a Mohawk term that means "boiling pot". To see boiling pots requires a 20-minute walk through town. Follow Church Street, turn left on Mohawk/Montgomery Street, then right on Moyer Street. Turn right on Floral Street. At the end follow a paved path to Canajoharie Creek where you will see a series of cascading waterfalls and several boiling pots, also known as kettle pots.

Historical Note: Canajoharie Library & Art Gallery, 1.5 blocks, has one of the finest small art galleries in the US. At the heart of its collection of 350 paintings by American artists is Winslow Homer oils and watercolors. The Village of Canajoharie has, architecturally, the most original, intact Erie Canal commercial district found on the Mohawk River.

Canajoharie Riverfront Park
Photo courtesy Rich & Sue Freeman,
m/v Choices

Library & Art Gallery, built in 1924
Photo courtesy Tug44.org

Mile 60.61, **Bridge E-24, State Route 10** (30.00')

Mile 60.95, **Lock E14, Canajoharie** (8') (R&P).
Pleasure craft are no longer permitted to tie up on the wall above this lock due to the adjacent unguarded railroad crossing. Docking is restricted to commercial vessels.

Mile 63.87, **Bridge E-25, State Route 80** (23.50')

Mile 64.30, **Lock E15, Fort Plain** (8') (R), **Free Dock.** Tie up east or west of lock on south wall. Short walls. At the end of the west wall there is a small embayment with room for one vessel. Electricity is available. Walk east on lock access road 0.5 mile to River Street and turn right (south). Restaurant, supermarket, hardware (0.7 miles) post office, Family Dollar (0.8 miles) store, laundry, bank, coffee shop, and Chinese Restaurant (1 mile). **Historical Note.** The remains of Fort Plain and the Fort Plain Museum are on the south bank about ½ mile west of Lock 15. It is a nice walk. Ask the lockmaster about directions and hours. Closed on Mondays.

Mile 64.36, **Anchorage.** Leave the Erie Canal at G "385" and proceed up the creek along Abeel Island. Anchor in 7 to 14 feet of water across from the Otsquago Fish & Game Club.

Mile 69.48, **St. Johnsville Municipal Marina,** (518-568-7406, G,D,P). 30/50A electric, laundry and showers. On the north wall in basin in St. Johnsville at R420. Water 10' at short wall. Nearby shopping includes a supermarket, several restaurants, and a liquor store. Free concerts on Monday night during the summer.

St. Johnsville Marina

Mile 69.57, **Bridge E-26A, Bridge St** (24.90')

Mile 70 to 72, **Historical Note.** Just east of Lock E16 remains of the old Erie Canal are visible on the south bank. West of Lock 16 remains can be seen on the north bank.

Mile 71.02, **Lock E16, St Johnsville** (20') (R), **Free Dock.** Tie up east or west of lock on south or north wall. Quiet, scenic and rural. **Anchorage.** Just east of the lock the Mohawk River rejoins the canal from the north. Proceed a short distance (not more than 50 yards) up the Mohawk and anchor in 6 to 8 feet of water. Area is also used by boats waiting for the lock.

Guard Gate 3
Photo courtesy of Tug44.org

Mile 71.45, **Bridge E-27, River Rd** (23.16')

Mile 72.53, **Bridge E-28, River Rd** (29.43')

Mile 74.54, **Guard Gate 3, Indian Castle**

Mile 74.94, **Bridge E-29, Lansing Rd** (24.00')

Mile 77.24, **Herkimer Home, Free Dock:** 60-foot floating dock, no services.

Historical Note: There is a nice museum here with history about the Revolutionary War and a collection of furniture from that period. General Nicholas Herkimer, famous for winning the Battle of Oriskany, is honored with a 60-foot obelisk.

Mile 78.87, **Bridge E-30A, SR 169** (32.39')

Lock 17 at Little Falls

Mile 78.99, **Lock E17, Little Falls** (40') (R). Westbound vessels must tie up to the south wall while traversing the lock. This is the largest single step lock on the Erie Canal. The east gate of Lock 17 is pulled up over the canal and you enter by taking your boat under this gate. (You will get wet!) **Free Dock.** Overnight tie up east of the lock on south lock wall under bridge E-30A. Because you are so low in the valley, the train and road noise is not bad here. There is some turbulence from the lock. It is a 20-minute walk to town. Ask the lockmaster about walking to Moss Island to view water sculptured rock formations over a million years old.

Historical Note. Lock 17 is impressive. Not only is it the highest lift lock on the Erie Canal it is believed to be one of only two locks in north America where the entrance gate is lifted **above** the boater. The other is on the Ottawa River in Canada. Frequently you will hear people refer to this as the "highest lift lock". This is not true. There are many lift locks that routinely raise or lower boats 55, 65 and 85 feet. In fact, the Wilson Lock and Dam on the Tennessee River has a lift of 97 feet. But these locks have gates that swing open as the vessel enters. Only Lock 17 and the one in Canada, lift the gates above the boater, permitting vessels to enter with a clearance of about 20 feet.

m/v Last Dance in Lock 17
Photo Courtesy of Glen and Jill Moore

Mile 79.01, **Little Falls, Free Dock.** (Day stop only, no overnight). Tie up to north canal wall at short space provided by the city. Clearly marked, this space is 1/3 the way west between Lock E17 and Bridge E-32A. Short walk to town and supermarket, theater, restaurants, etc. Nice view of Little Falls rapids.

Mile 79.74, **Bridge E-32A, State Route 167** (23.00')

Mile 79.84, **Guard Gate 4, Little Falls**

Mile 80.10, **Little Falls Canal Harbor,**
(315-823-1453, P). Just west of Guard
Gate 4 on the south bank. The 1918
Barge canal terminal building has been
renovated to include the dockmasters
office, meeting room, showers, restrooms
and laundry. A nice fountain is adjacent
to the building. There is a 100' long
plastic floating dock at the east end of the
600' wall, with small plastic cleats
appropriate for smaller boats with 1/2"
lines. There are three power pedestals.
After the ramp up to the top of the wall,
there is another 100' of floating dock with
no power. The tall concrete wall to the
west is 400' long with three power
pedestals along the west end. There is one
more pedestal next to the building about
mid-section. All pedestals have on 30A
and one 50A outlet and water connections.
Water depth 10' at dockside. Open 7:30am
to 6pm during the summer with reduced
hours in the fall. In January 2021, the
transient rate was $1.00/ft., pump out
$5.00. Some restaurants will pick you and
your crew up, take you to the restaurant
and return you when you are finished
dining.

The terminal building at Little Falls.
Photo courtesy Tug44.org

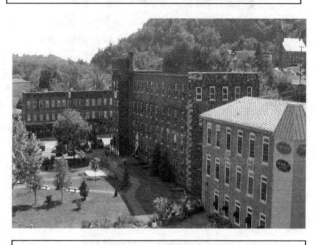

Canal Place in Little Falls
Photo Courtesy Tug44.org

Little Falls has much to offer. Within
walking distance you will find specialty
shops, hardware and lumber, pharmacies,
groceries, florists, antique shops and much more. A Farmer's Market is held every
Saturday morning from May through October and a Summer Concert Series presents free
open-air concerts on Wednesdays. Canal Days is celebrated in early August. For detailed
information of all that Little Falls offers, visit their website, www.littlefallsny.com
Many cruisers consider this to be one of the finest stops on the canal.

Mile 83.19, **Lock E18** (20') (R&C), **Free Dock.** Tie up east or west of lock on south wall. Short
walls.

Mile 86.36, **Bridge E-34A, Washington St** (21.50')

Mile 86.47, **Bridge E-34B, NYS Thruway** (29.90')

Mile 87.20, **Guard Gate 5, Herkimer**

Mile 87.37, **Herkimer**, **Free Dock:** 500' of wall in front of the restaurant and gift shop and 200' of floating dock just to the west. Water and power is not available. The center of the floating dock is reserved for a commercial boating enterprise. Lots of road noise. Inside the building on the east end is the gift shop, Gems Along the Mohawk, with a collection

of upscale gifts from over 50 vendors. **Note:** Depths of 6' or less reported in 2018. On the east end is the Waterfront Grille which is open for lunch and dinner. The area is famous for "Herkimer Diamonds", which are quartz crystals. You can take a taxi 6 miles north to visit one of the mines, which are open to the public. The mines come complete with museums. You can also rent tools to break off a few samples of "diamonds" for yourself, which you can keep as souvenirs.

Cross the bridge south for the Mohawk Restaurant and across the street the Factory Depot outlet store. The bridge is called the POW/MIA Remembrance Bridge.

Proceed north on Mohawk Street towards town 0.3 miles, under two bridges, and come to traffic light with the intersection of route 5. Head west on Caroline Street to the next light (total 0.5 miles). At the corner is McDonalds, pizzeria, KFC, and Waffle Works. Behind the McDonalds is a Wal-Mart Super Center. Just west of McDonalds is Agway where you can fill your propane tanks. (Wal-Mart is a total of 0.7 miles from the terminal)

The electrical equipment operating the locks is early 1900 vintage and is lovingly maintained by the lock personnel year-round.

North at the McDonald traffic light to the town of Herkimer. Along the way, Pizza Hut, Advance Auto Parts, Army Navy Surplus Store, Rite Aid Pharmacy and Burger King. At 0.9 miles from the terminal is the center of Herkimer. There isn't much in the way of shopping except a hardware store and some restaurants. Continue north for Kmart, Ponderosa Steak House, Arby's and finally a large Hannaford Supermarket. Hannaford is a total of 1.2 miles from the terminal.

Mile 89.07, **Ilion Marina and RV Park,** (315-894-9421, G,D,P,Wi-Fi) 600' wall with 6 electric stands 30/50A, showers and laundry. Rate in January 2021 was $1/ft. which included electric, water and WiFi. There is a popular café' on site with sandwiches and ice cream.

It's a short walk to Aldi Supermarket, Rite-Aid Drugs, McDonalds, Stewart's, and the Remington Arms Factory. Annual Ilion Days celebrated in mid-July.

Historical Note. The Remington Arms Museum and Country Store is open weekdays 8am to 5pm. An interesting display of guns and other bits of history plus videos of the manufacturing process awaits the visitor. Ask the marina manager for directions.

Mile 89.15, **Bridge E-37A, Central Ave** (21.70')
Mile 91.60, **Bridge E-38, Railroad St** (34.40')

Mile 91.64, **Frankfort Harbor Marina**, in an embayment on the south side, has 12 floating slips without water or electric. Town is just a few blocks away.

Mile 92.51, **Bridge E-39, Moss Rd** (21.88')

Mile 94.92, **Bridge E-40, railroad** (21.37') **Note:** Vertical clearance will be reduced when the chamber of Lock E19 is emptied but it is not an issue.

Mile 95.04, **Lock E19, Frankfort** (21')(R&P), **Free Dock.** Tie up west of lock on the short south lock wall. Train transits east end of lock so some noise, but tolerable.

Mile 97.54, **Bridge E-42, Dyke Rd** (22.20')

Mile 100.85, **Utica,** Utica Marina (city owned), $1.00/ft. includes water and electric. Terminal is on the south shore east of Bridge E-44A and adjacent to the Aqua Vino Restaurant and Lounge (315-732-0116), which collects the fee. Floating dock (120' has 30A power, high wall (250') has 50A. During heavy rains debris from small creek across canal from marina may wash up against vessels.

Utica Marina
Photo courtesy Tug44.org

South on Genesee Street 0.5 miles is Wendy's, McDonalds, Denny's, Delmonico Steak House, Dunkin Donuts, and Friendly Ice Cream. At 0.7 miles south you will find the train station, which is 100 years old with massive marble pillars and curved wooden benches. Well worth the visit.

North on Genesee Street under two bridges 0.5 miles and turn east. You will find North Utica Shopping Center with Price Chopper Supermarket, Dollar Tree, Bank ATM, Eckert Drug Store, Burger King, and etc.

Tour the Saranac Brewery which is less than a two mile walk from the marina. Admission is $5 per person, but you sample the brew!

Mile 100.54, **Bridge E-43, Leland Ave** (22.28')

Mile 100.90, **Bridge E-44A, Genesee St** (22.20')

Mile 101.67, **Utica Harbor Lock.** On south bank east of bridge E-44B on a side channel. Closed to all vessels. You can tie up to widely spaced bollards on the short lock wall just west of lock entrance, **Free Dock.** Two mile walk south to city of Utica.

Historical Note. Utica was the terminus of the Chenango Canal which connected Utica with Binghamton, NY to the south and on to Waverly, NY on the Pennsylvania and New York border at the head of the navigable Susquehanna River; about 80 miles away. This canal has been abandoned.

Miles 101.80 to 101.97, **Bridges E-44B** (22.20'), **exit ramp, E-44C** (22.40'), **State Route 8 & 12, E-44D, exit ramp** (23.10')

Mile 102.44, **Bridge E-46, railroad** (22.17')

Mile 104.40, **Bridge E-47A, Mohawk St** (22.30')

Mile 104.62, **Bridge E-47B, NYS Thruway** (22.24')

Mile 105.32, **Lock E20, Whitesboro** (16')(R). **Free Dock.** Tie up east or west of lock on very long south wall. West of lock adjacent to the north wall is a small park with a picnic shelter, restrooms, tables, grills and a water faucet. Small park and trail off the south wall as well.

Miles 105.63 to 113.78, **Bridges E-48A, State Rt 291** (22.50'), **E-49, Oriskany Rd** (23.20'), **E-50, railroad** (22.50'), **Guard Gate 6, E-50A, Rome Arterial** (39.10')

Mile 114.79, **Bridge E-51** (23.40')

Mile 114.97, **Rome, Bellamy Harbor Park, Free Dock.** Tie up to north terminal wall between bridges E-51 and E-52A. On the east end the pilings and wooden wall behind the old terminal building are in very bad shape. This area is primarily used by canal corporation barges and you should avoid it. A 200' fixed dock is at the west end. There is no electric service. There are two short (50 and 40 feet) floating docks at the west end without power or water. Check the depth; in 2019 reported to be 4 feet. There is a picnic area at the east end. The Navigation Center hosts bathrooms, showers,

Bellamy Harbor Park
Photo courtesy City of Rome

laundry, and a community room.

To go to town, you have two choices. Turn right out of the park and left on Mill Street. Walk north on Mill Street 0.4 miles to Dominick Street. Turn left/west on Dominick and walk 0.3 miles to Fort Stanwix, passing a gas station with a convenience store, an Italian Market with pastas, sausages, etc. and a pizzeria. Pass Fort Stanwix on the south side and you find a large Ace Hardware. Continue west 0.2 miles on Erie Blvd and find Freedom Plaza with Tops Supermarket, ALDI's, Staples, Rite Aid, Walgreen's, and Dollar Tree. Total distance from free dock to Freedom Plaza is 1 mile. Or, turn left out of park, go over footbridge, under the highway overpass and turn right onto Erie Blvd. Via this route it is about 0.8 miles to Freedom Plaza, but you will find a propane fill at U-Haul on Erie Blvd at 0.25 miles. The Veschio Restaurant in the Franklin Hotel reportedly has very good food at reasonable prices in a casual atmosphere. The Savoy Restaurant on Dominick Street serves Italian food.

Rome celebrates Canal Fest in early August and the Taste of the Arts Festival near the end of September.

Historical Note. Located in downtown Rome is the restored Fort Stanwix, an excellent reproduction of a Revolutionary War wooden fort. This fort takes up an entire city block and is a must see for those interested in history. General John Stanwix built this fort in 1758 to protect the important portage between the Mohawk River and Wood Creek. Under siege by the British in August 1777, the commander was able to hold out against a force three times as large as his. General Herkimer was ambushed trying to reach Fort Stanwix, to provide relief. Finally, the siege was broken when General Benedict Arnold approached with a small band of reinforcements. The British were deceived into thinking it was a much larger band and withdrew to Canada. Allow for about 3 hours to see the museum and all that the fort has to offer. **Free admission.** Schedule your day right and enjoy lunch in one of the nearby restaurants or fast food stores.

Historical Note. Construction on the original Erie Canal started near Rome in July 1817 at a place now called the Erie Canal Village. This 1840s village has been faithfully reproduced and provides an interesting insight in to life in the early days of the Erie Canal. Open Wednesday to Sunday. A section of the original canal has been restored and you can ride on a replica of an old canal boat. There is much to see and do. Unfortunately, the Erie Canal Village is about 5 miles from the terminal in Rome and not recommended as a walk. Consider a taxi if you want to visit this interesting site.

Restored Fort Stanwix at Rome, NY

Mile 115.05, **Guard Gate 7**

Miles 115.08 to 119.85, **Bridges E-52A, Erie Blvd East** (33.75'), **E-55, South James St** (24.25'), **E-57, Stony Creek Rd** (22.60')

Mile 121.38, **Historical Note.** On the south bank, at green marker 657, a junction lock from the old Erie Canal has been made into a dry lock. Short wall west of lock to tie up to. No services.

Mile 122.10, **Bridge E-58A, New London** (24.04')
Mile 123.42, **Lock E21, New London** (25')(R), **Free Dock.** This is the first lock going down when headed west. You can tie up east of lock to south lock wall. Quiet rural setting. In fact it is so quiet here one boater commented, "city folks won't be able to sleep here." **Bridge E-59** clearance is 23.18' **Note:** Docking is not permitted between Locks E21 and E22 due to fluctuating water levels.

Mile 124.74, **Lock E22, Sylvan Beach** (25')(R). Tie to north wall; no lines on south wall. **Free Dock.** Tie off on west wall. No services.

Mile 126.04, **Bridge E-60, Higginsville Rd** (23.17')

Mile 128.19, **Bridge E-61, Cove Rd** (23.00')

Mile 128.92, **Mariner's Landing,** (315-762-0112, G,D). On north bank west of G683.

Mile 128.92, **Holmes Marina,** (315-400-5801). In basin on south bank west of G683. Travel Lift.

Historical Note - This is where the Old Oneida Canal entered Wood Creek. The Old Oneida Canal ran SE from this point to Higginsville on the original Erie canal. This canal operated from 1835 to 1863. The Old Oneida Canal was closed in 1863 because the wooden locks had deteriorated to the point that they were unsafe. Although these locks were supposed to be replaced by stone locks it never happened. The Old Oneida Canal was never reopened after 1863. Instead the New Oneida Canal opened in 1877, and started at Durnhamville, some distance to the south. The New Oneida Canal entered Oneida Lake at South Bay in the SE corner of Oneida Lake. In 1915 the Erie Canal was enlarged and made into the New York Barge Canal. This canal entered Oneida Lake at Sylvan Beach and the original Erie Canal which passed south of Oneida Lake was closed cutting off canal traffic to Durnhamville and Syracuse to the south of Oneida Lake.

Mile 129.15, **Snug Harbour Marina,** (315-762-5104, G, P) In basin on south bank east of Bridge E-63.

Mile 129.18, **Bridge E-63, State Route 13**
   (24.22')

Mile 129.34, **Sylvan Beach**, **Free Dock.** Tie up
   east or west of bridge E-63 to north town
   wall. 700' long wall east of bridge and
   500' wall west of bridge E-63. No
   electric or water. There is also a 500'
   wall on the south side west of the bridge.
      Amusement park, swim beach,
   restaurants, laundromat, post office,
   ATM, and pizzerias all within 5 blocks
   north of wall. Provisions available only
   from convenience stores. On Thursday
   nights during the summer, antique car enthusiasts with their "trophy cars" gather by the
   amusement park.
      Sylvan Beach celebrates Canal Fest early in August.

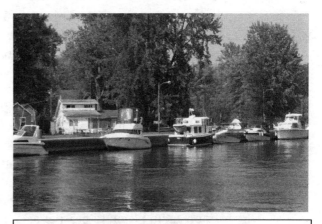

Terminal wall at Sylvan Beach
Photo courtesy Tug44.org

Mile 129.89 to 149.96. **Oneida Lake.** The largest body of water on the Erie Canal. There are
   several marinas along both the north and south bank, but the specifics are not listed in
   this book as cruisers rarely use these facilities, since they are out of the way. There are
   marinas on the Erie Canal just east and west of Oneida Lake and they are listed. The GPS
   coordinates at the east end of the lake just south of R106 are N43° 11.342 and W75°
   44.330. Midpoint at G125 the coordinates are N43° 12.488 and W75° 56.064. The west
   end of the lake in the channel at bridge E-63A is at N43° 14.259 and W76° 07.271.
      This lake does not have a speed limit, but you are responsible for your wake. Local
   constables patrol both ends and frequently pull over boaters who cause problems on the
   open lake.

Mile 150.00, **Trade A Yacht Marina,** (315-676-3531, G,D,P) On north bank just east of bridge
   E-63A.

 Mile 150 to mile 172. A great many private docks will be found alongside this stretch of the
   Erie Canal. Plan on going slow for this 22 miles at a no wake speed. Local homeowners
   expect it and are not reluctant to call the police for vessels creating a serious wake.

Mile 150.06, **Bridge E-63A, Interstate 81** (23.50')

Mile 150.50**, Brewerton, Free Dock.** A 300´ dock is on the north shoreline. Tie on either side.
   One power pedestal on the west end of the dock is for use by canal maintenance crews.
   The 48- hour limit applies. Waterfront Tavern adjacent to the dock. Two blocks north to
   propane tank exchange, restaurants and convenience store. Or tie up just west of bridge
   E-64 on south wall. Two blocks south to restaurants, Family Dollar Store, pizzeria, new
   library with Internet access, and pharmacy. Seven blocks south to mini mall with
   McDonalds, Dunkin Donuts, Subway, pizzeria, liquor store, Chinese takeout, coin

laundry, and Kinney Drugs, which has dairy products, and a well-stocked marine store, Marine 2000. A total of 1 mile from the free dock next to the mini mall on the south side of the road is the post office. A Walmart Supercenter, Wegman's Supermarket is about 6 miles south on Route 11.

Historical Note. The original Erie Canal passed to the south of Lake Oneida. Remember that originally the canal was nothing more than a ditch which mules and horses pulled barges through. Lake Oneida was too large and there were no self-propelled boats on the canal then. Brewerton was nearly forgotten as trade and boats passed to the south. As time went on, self-propelled boats were introduced to the canal and in 1917 when the Erie Canal was enlarged and relocated; it passed right through Lake Oneida and Brewerton. Brewerton again began to prosper as a boat-building center. Today, it is one of the best-equipped areas on the Erie Canal to have maintenance performed on your boat.

Mile 150.58, **Bridge E-64, US Route 11** (23.50')

Mile 150.72, **Bridge E-65, railroad** (21.72')

Mile 150.83, **Brewerton Boat Yard,** (315-676-3762, G,D,P,WiFi).On south bank just west of RR bridge and G147. Large service yard, ships store.

Mile 151.10, **Ess-Kay Yards, Inc,** (315-676-2711, G,D,P,WiFi). On south bank opposite R150. Large service yard, ships store. The town of Brewerton is only a few blocks to the east.

Mile 151.64, **Winter Harbor Marina,** (315-676-9276, G,D,P,WiFi). On north bank opposite G151. Large service yard, ships store.

Mile 152.90, **Bridge E-66, Caughdenoy Rd** (23.50')

Mile 153.65, **Lock E23, Brewerton** (7')(R). This is the last lock down when headed west. **Free Dock.** Tie up west of lock on south wall. Picnic tables, barbecue, etc. in park on south side. Or you can tie up east of lock on new high wooden 250' dock on south bank. Quiet rural setting. Lock tours conducted.

Mile 154.01, **Bridge E-67, Black Creek Rd** (23.10')

Mile 156.50, **Bridge E-68, Morgan Rd (CR 9),** (22.80')

Guard Gate, Lock E23

Mile 158.18, **Pirate's Cove Marina,** (315-695-3901, G,P). On south bank behind an island opposite R200.

Mile 158.31, **Bridge E-69, Horseshoe Island Rd** (22.40')

Mile 159.40, **Bridge E-69A, State Rd 481** (22.70')

Mile 160.32, **Bridge E-70, railroad** (22.64')

Mile 160.34, **Bridge E-71, Count Route 57** (22.62')

Mile 160.45, **Canal Junction**. Vessels going north on the Oswego Canal leave the Erie Canal here. See Chapter 5 of this book. There is a **Free Dock** here on the south bank just west of Bridge E-71. The wall is very low here and there are no services.

Chapter 4

The Western Erie Canal

This chapter deals with the Erie Canal west from the Junction of the Oswego Canal at Three Rivers and includes the junction of the Cayuga Seneca Canal and the terminus at Tonawanda, NY (Buffalo). All comments below are referenced by mile marked west from the beginning of the Erie Canal at Waterford, NY.

Caution – Remember that the clearance of the New York Canal System is only 15' 5" west of Three Rivers. This also includes the Cayuga-Seneca Canal. Pool levels between locks can vary by a few inches to a few feet after rain. Always watch your clearance and do not "assume" you can get through all bridges because you are less than 15' 5". Most bridges do not have sight gauges.

Mile 162.39, **Bridge E-72, Belgium Rd, State Route 31** (21.31')

Mile 167.10, **Bridge E-73, State Route 370** (22.87')

Mile 166.18, **Lake Onondaga.** Divert south 3 miles to Liverpool on Lake Onondaga and tie up at The Onondaga Lake Park Marina. It is a short walk to grocery, restaurants, and drug store. Visit the interesting Salt Museum in town or take public bus to Syracuse to visit Erie Canal Museum. Post office and supermarket within 3 blocks.

For the more adventurous, explore Syracuse by boat. Proceed south to the end of the lake at N43º 04.164 and W76º 10.840. Enter the old Syracuse terminal basin. **Caution:** Channel depths reported to be 6 feet or less and less than 5 feet in the basin. Check the NY Canals website for current levels. Tie up at the 1000' terminal wall with floating dock on the south side of the basin. Landscaped with large building. Eight 30A marine stands with water. No adjacent shopping or stores, however a major redevelopment project is underway. The Aloft Syracuse Inner Harbor Hotel is on site and condos are under construction. Restaurant and grocery about one-quarter mile away.

Historical Note. The original Erie Canal passed right through downtown Syracuse. As such, much of the city developed around it. Today the canal has been filled in and the street thus created named Erie Boulevard. The Erie Canal Museum in Syracuse is built in one of the original "weigh stations" on Erie Boulevard. Here boats were actually weighed on a beam and balance to determine how much tariff they should pay for using the canal. Boats were weighed and certified empty once per year. Then whenever weighed later on during the year, the difference between the current weight and the certified empty weight was the weight of the cargo.

An interesting story is told in the museum about one captain who hid ballast in his "empty" boat. He then had it weighed with this extra dead weight aboard. After that when hauling cargo, he removed the extra ballast and of course his cargo appeared to weigh less than it actually did. The authorities were not too happy with this captain when they discovered his deceit. This and many more interesting stories, facts, and displays await the visitor lucky enough to visit the Erie Canal Museum in Syracuse.

Mile 167.40, **Cold Springs Harbor Marina**, (315-622-2211, G,P). On the north bank behind Klein Island at the junction of the Onondaga Lake cutoff. A fleet of rental canal boats is maintained here. Marina can accommodate vessels up to 45'.

Mile 167.88, **J&S Marine, (**315-622-1095, G,P) On the north bank east of R286.

Mile 170.51, **Bridge E-77, railroad** (19.57')

Mile 172.36, **Bridge E-78, Syracuse St** (18.80')

Mile 172. 42, **Lock E24, Baldwinsville** (11')(R) Tie up east or west of the lock on south wall. Restaurants, convenience store, pharmacy, bank, hardware, liquor store, and video store north of lock. East of the lock there is 100 feet of wall with no services. Canal park with 1000' wall and 200' floating dock on south bank west of lock. Along the wall there are 7 pedestals with 30/50A service and water. On the floating dock there a 6 pedestals with 30/50A service and water. Dockage is free. Electric is $5/night for 30A and $10/night for 50A. It is a one mile walk to shopping plaza on south bank. On the north bank, which is actually Paper Mill Island, is a 120' floating dock with no water or electric

Village of Baldwinsville Docks
Photo courtesy Jana & Mike Kent, Lady J

service.. Located on the island is the Budweiser Amphitheater and a former grain mill converted into a conference center. There are restrooms and showers ($0.25) here but they may be locked at night. Check with lockmaster. Shoaling along this wall has been reported.

On Saturday nights in season free concerts are held at the amphitheater and vessels are not permitted to tie to the 200' wall during the concerts.

Baldwinsville celebrates Seneca River Days in mid-July and Golden Harvest Festival early September.

Historical Note. Just west of Lock 24 on the Island on the north side of the canal is an operating electric power plant. Still operated today as an independent power generating plant fueled by the waters of the Seneca River. On the rare occasion when the operator is there, she will be glad to show you the workings of the plant.

Mile 173.26, **Coopers Marina, Inc,** (315-635-7371, G,P) 30/50A electric service. On the north bank west of R336.

Mile 174.06, **Bridge E-78A, State Route 690** (23.30')

Mile 176.81, Rocks. **Caution** – Near buoys R370 and R372 just outside the channel is a rocky areas. Do not drift out of the channel.

Mile 180.82, **Bridge E-79, Plainville Rd** (20.57')

Mile 182.00, east bound vessels turn to port at G409. Seneca River continues straight.

Mile 183.28, **Cross Lake**, Caution: Buoy G419 may be positioned further to the north of Little Island than shown on the canal system chart. Depths drop to 8 to 9 feet when leaving the lake. Charts may show deeper water.

Mile 184.70, **Bridge E-80, River Rd** (25.40')

Mile 185.53, **Seneca River. Caution:** Shoaling to 7' on the north side between R434 and G435.

Mile 186.60, **Bridge E-81, Bonta Rd** (19.68')

Mile 188.87, **Bridge E-83, State Route 34** (25.30')

Mile 188.90, **Free Dock.** Tie up west of Bridge E-83 to the Village of Weedsport Terminal Wall on the south shore. Short wall, fixed bollards, two or three boats. Wall is high and rough. Use several fenders. No services. Restaurant, Devaney's Riverside Grill, next to the wall.

Miles 192.72 to 197.03, **Bridges E-84, O'Neil Rd** (20.63'), **E-85, State Route 38** (25.00'), **E-86, Howland Island Rd** (20.51')

Mile 197.06, **Bridge E-87, railroad** (21.19')

Mile 197.56, **West of Bridge E-87.** Reported 7' depth from bridge to G517 and 8' to R518.

Mile 200.11, **Bridge E-90, State Route 31** (25.80')

Mile 200.82, **Historical Note.** On both sides of the canal at R538, the remains of the Montezuma (Richmond) Aqueduct can be seen, where the canal of 1862 crossed the Seneca River. This aqueduct was 900 feet long. When the present Erie Canal was constructed in the Seneca River the center section of this aqueduct was removed.

Mile 201.38, **Canal Junction**. Vessels desiring to explore Cayuga or Seneca lakes go south here on the Cayuga-Seneca canal. See Chapter 6 of this book. Pay attention to your charts. When westbound, slow down after Bridge E-90 and prepare to turn at channel marker G541. When eastbound, slow down after Lock E25 and prepare to turn at G547. Junction well-marked. When heading east and turning south, the buoys reverse...red right, green left. Also, be aware of some shoaling when southbound.

Mile 203.11, **Lock E25, May's Point** (6')(R), **Free Dock.** Tie up east or west of lock on long south wall. Quiet rural setting. Small bait shop with snacks ¼ mile south. **Bridge E-91, State Route 89** (25.55')

Mile 205.59, **Bridge E-92, Armitage Rd (County Line)** (18.45')

Mile 208.94, **Lock E26, Clyde** (6')(R), **Free Dock.** Tie up east or west of lock on short south wall. Quiet rural setting.

Mile 209.36, **Bridge E-93, railroad** (16.13').

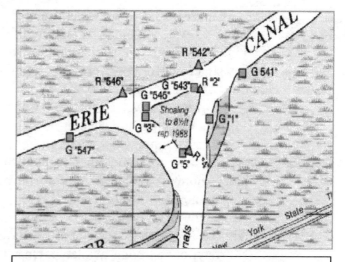

Junction of Erie and Cayuga-Seneca Canals

Mile 211.26, **Clyde, Free Dock.** Tie up to a fixed bulkhead (75') with two small floating Docks (40') on the south bank east of the Glasgow Street bridge, E-94. Room for three boats, 48 hour limit. Water and electric available from two posts at each end of the wall by the gangway to the docks. Free pump-out at west end of docks. Town located on the north side of the canal. Noisy train traffic.

Mile 211.32, **Bridge E-94, State Route 414 (Glascow Street)** (20.54')

Mile 217.76, **Bridge E-96, Lyons-Marengo Rd (Creager)** (18.58')

Mile 218.67, **Bridge E-97, abandoned railroad** (17.72') **Caution:** Shoaling to 6' on the north side until past R658.

Mile 219.94, **Bridge E-99, railroad** (18.20') **Caution:** Shoaling to 7' on the south side until past G665. **Note:** Multiple tracks.

Mile 220.27, **Bridge E-99A, State Route 31** (25.67')

Mile 220.77, **Bridge E-100, Geneva St** (19.86')

Mile 220.82, **Lyons, Free Dock.** Tie up east of lock on either north (preferred) or south wall. The north wall is 500' and features 30/50A electric. There is also a 80' floating dock with a pump-out. It does not have electric. WiFi available.

Caution - There are water drainpipes along the wall. An amazing amount of water and debris comes out of these pipes from the city streets when it rains. **Do Not** tie up in front of these pipes.

Showers and water at the fire department adjacent to the dock. Registration also. Restaurants, liquor store, bank, pizzeria, post office, laundromat and other shops within 3 blocks north. All village facilities shown on map on north wall at east end.

On the south bank, there is a long wall with 12 15A outlets located 65' from wall. No water or restrooms available. On south bank there is a McDonalds, ATM, Chinese restaurant, Kinney Pharmacy, propane exchange and Santelli Lumberyard. South to route 31 and west 0.3 miles to ALDI, a large discount supermarket. Ice is available at 3 locations 1 block north and south of canal. Farmers Market on Saturday at the Village Square Park. Enjoy the many painted murals throughout the village.

Finally, tie up west of lock on north wall at Abbey Park. No electric.

Free dock at Lyons
Photo courtesy Tug44.org

Historical note: During early canal days Lyons was a major exporter of peppermint. Visit the Wayne County Historical Society Museum in an 1854 sheriff's home with attached jail. The old E56 lock is located nearby.

Mile 220.99, **Lock 27, Lyons** (12')(R) **Bridge E-101, Leach Rd** just past the lock has a vertical clearance of 18'. The pipeline bridge is 30'.

Mile 222.22, **Bridge E-104, Drydock Rd** (18.85')

Mile 222.27, **Lock E28A, Lyons** (20')(R), **Free Dock.** Tie up on south bank, east of lock on short wall or west of lock on long wall. Water. Active canal dry dock. Walmart 3 miles west on Route 31.

Mile 223.70, **Bridge E-105, County House Rd** (16.90')

Mile 224.65, **Bridge E-106, multi-track railroad** (16.37')

Mile 226.21, **Bridge E-108, Clinton St** (16.95')

Canal Corp. Dry Dock at Lock E28A
Photo courtesy Tug44.org

Mile 226.25, **Lock E28B, Newark** (12')(R), Lock walls very rough. Old lock 59 adjacent to lock.

Mile 226.38, **Bridge E-109, old railroad** (27.99')

Mile 226.66, **Bridge E-110, East Ave** (18.00')

Mile 226.67, **Newark Terminal, Free Dock.** North wall has 600' wall with 100' floating dock with a verified 8' alongside. South wall has 600' wall a posted depth of 4'. North wall has 7 power stands with 15A/30A/50A service. Picnic tables. Free pump out. Free WiFi. Free showers and laundry in lower level of dockmasters building. Air-conditioned! Ice and propane exchange ½ block north. Check in at the Chamber of Commerce office, located upstairs in the dockmaster's building.

Newark's Dockmasters office
Photo courtesy Tug44.org

Newark celebrates Newark Fest each year in early June with open-air booths and fun for all. Farmers Market 0.5 miles west on Westshore Blvd Thursdays June to September. Band concert in Central Park 7:30-8:30pm July and August.

On the south bank Eckerd Drug, Save-a-Lot Supermarket, city library and several nice shops and restaurants. South of canal east on 31 is a Dunkin Donuts, convenience store and diner.

The murals painted on the stone arch bridge are part of an ongoing project called Mural Mania that will result in murals depicting historic scenes along 50 miles of the canal.

Historical Note. Visit the Hoffman Clock Museum located in the public library on High Street, two blocks south. Free admission. On Tuesday mornings a curator is present.

Newark Murals
Photo courtesy Don Robertson, M/V Cygnus

Miles 226.79 to 232.54, **Bridges E-111, Main St** (17.68'), **E-112, Edgett St** (18.01'), **E-113, Whitbeck Rd** (17.68'), **E-114, Port Gibson** (17.68'), **E-115, Galloway Rd** (22.70')

Mile 234.51, **Palmyra, Free Dock.** There is a terminal wall under **Bridge E-116** on the south bank. West 1.5 blocks on Canal Street to Laundromat. Walk to Palmyra 2 blocks south and the main shopping area with Dollar General, Rite Aid pharmacy, and IGA Supermarket. Not the preferred stop. See mile 235.03.

Mile 235.03, **Palmyra, Free Dock.** Port of Palmyra Marina on the south side immediately east of Bridge E-117 with three 30A power stands, several water faucets, and 2 pump outs.

Use your adapter. Restrooms and showers at the picnic pavilion. This small man-made basin juts into the south shore and provides 6 - 7' of water alongside the dock. Small restaurant at the end of the pier. While this stop is closest to the town of Palmyra, it is not closest to the IGA Supermarket. See mile 234.51 for that.

Port of Palmyra Marina
Photo courtesy Tug44.org

Walk south on Division Street about three blocks to main street Palmyra. In town you will find several museums, Family Dollar Store, multiple restaurants, pizzerias, Laundromat, fudge store, ice cream shop, bank, and shops all within 4 blocks of the dock. Walking east on main street takes you past restaurants, shops, filling station, and at about ½ mile from the dock the PO. At about 1 mile you find a Dollar General, Rite Aid and the IGA Supermarket. Canal Town Days celebrated in mid-September. Post Office zip **14522**.

Historical Note. Joseph Smith founded the Church of Jesus Christ of Latter Day Saints in Palmyra in 1830. You can visit his home on Stafford Street 2 miles south. Now a museum, it is open daily to visitors at no charge.

Palmyra is noted for an intersection where there are 4 churches, one on each corner. It is at the junction of Route 21 and 31(Main Street). Palmyra claims to have the only such junction in the world!

Mile 235.06, **Bridge E-117, Division St** (17.64')

Mile 235.28, **Bridge E-118, County Route 210** (17.93')

Mile 236.04, **Lock E29, Palmyra** (16')(R), **Free Dock.** Lock walls are deteriorating and need repair. Use extra fenders. Tie up east (preferred) or west of lock on south wall. Canal park at lock. In the park is the Aldrich Change Bridge, which allowed for mules to transfer from one side of the canal to the other. The town of Palmyra is a 0.8-mile walk east with drug store, post office, bank (ATM), restaurants, and video store. A total of 1.4 miles east brings you to the main shopping area described at mile 234.5. From this lock west, there is a complete bicycle path all the way to Buffalo, NY. (100 miles)

Mile 236.54, **Bridge E-119, Walworth Rd** (16.25'). Small inlets on the north side are remains of the old canal (Clinton's Ditch).

Mile 237.98, **Old Lock 60 Park.** 35' floating dock on north shore. There are no cleats or rings so you have to tie up to the pipes that hold the dock in place. Depths reported to be 8'.

Mile 238.34, **Bridge E-120, O'Neill Rd** (16.17')

Mile 238.59, **Bridge E-120A, pipeline** (21.00')

Mile 238.93, **Bridge E-121, State Route 350** (20.60')

Mile 239.02, **Lock E30 Macedon** (16')(R), **Free Dock.** Tie up east (preferred) or west of lock on south wall. Canal park west of lock. Portable toilets, but there are two water spigots for filling your tanks. To get to town go south ¼ mile on route 350 to Route 31 and turn east where you will find convenience store, pizzeria, gas station and sub shop. A total of ¾ miles east from lock you will find a strip mall on Route 31 with McDonalds, bank, movie, and restaurant.

> **Historical Note.** Walk east across Route 350 and visit the old lock 61 from the 1862 canal. Ask the Lock 30 lockmaster for instructions. Old lock 60 is visible at mile 237.8 east of Lock 30. Between Lock E30 and Bridge E-122 you can see remnants of the original canal on the south side.

Mile 239.98, **Bridge E-122, Canandaigua Rd** (15.60')

Mile 240.13, **Mid-Lakes Erie Macedon Landing Marina,** (315-986-3011, G,D,P, WiFi). Lockmaster Canal Boats may be chartered here.

Mile 242.07, **Bridge E-123, Wayneport Rd** (15.97')

Mile 242.10, **End of day marks**. **Note -** There are no numbered day marks west of Beacon R810.

Mile 244.33, **Bridge E-124, Lyndon Rd** (20.30')

Miles 245.86 to 246.52, **Bridges E-125A, pedestrian (Perinton Hike/Bikeway Trail)** (17.29'), **E-126, Turk Hill Rd** (16.10'), **E-127, Parker St** (16.10')

Mile 246.58, **Fairport.** East of Main Street (E-128) Lift Bridge on south and north wall there are 30A electric stands. Six stands on the south and six on the north. West of Main Street Lift Bridge tie up to dock on north bank with 15/30A electric and water. East of the Parker Street Bridge (E-127) there are four 30A stands and a pump out. Dockage fee (sliding scale up to $17.00 in January 2021) includes the use of handicap accessible rest room, showers and pump out.

This is a very popular stop. Fairport is a very friendly tourist town with many shops and good restaurants. WiFi available, dockmaster has password. Ice and laundry 3 blocks north of lift bridge. Canal Days celebrated in early June. Farmers market on Saturday mornings during summer. Concerts are held at the Gazebo on Thursdays during June, July and August.

Fairport town dock, a very popular stop

Historical Note. The lift bridge (E-128 at mile 246.67) is in the Guinness Book of Records for several reasons. One end is higher than the other, it is built on a slant and no two angles on the entire bridge are the same.

Mile 246 to 341, **Historical Note.** This portion of the Erie Canal, about 100 miles, most closely resembles the original Erie Canal as a ditch dug through the landscape with a towpath on both sides. There are many places to stop and miles of walking/bicycling paths along the old towpath. Get used to going slow, stopping often, taking in the sights, and seeing joggers, walkers and bicyclers.

Mile 247.61, **Bridge E-129, W. Church St** (16.10')

Mile 247.65, **Perinton Park, Free Dock.** Tie up on north wall at park. Water depth under 5' at wall. No overnight docking.

Mile 249.12, **Bridge E-130, Aryault Rd** (16.58')

Mile 249.47, **Bridge E-131, Palmyra Rd** (16.10')

Mile 249.96, **Bushnell's Basin Guard Gate**

Bushnell's Basin Guard Gate
Photo courtesy Tug44.org

Mile 250.29, **Bridge E-131A, I- 490** (20.15')

Mile 250.60, **Bridge E-133, Marsh Rd** (16.14')

Mile 250.66, **Bushnell's Basin.** Tie up west of Marsh Road fixed bridge to 250' floating
dock. Four power pedestals with 2 30A and 2 50A per pedestal, water, pump-out,
restrooms with showers. Dockage fee (January 2021) is a sliding scale up to $11. Pay at
Steamer's Hess Station. Ice available at Hess. Small strip mall west of bridge on south
bank with Rite Aid, bank ATM, and liquor store. Small shopping strip south bank of
canal east of bridge with ice cream shop, drug store, and restaurants, including
Richardson's Canal House. Built as a tavern in 1818, it is the oldest original inn on the
Erie Canal. **Note:** Be prepared for a lot of casual pedestrian traffic.

Mile 251.81, **Great Embankment Park.** Small dock with no services and no overnight. The
vertical concrete walls magnify wakes and cause endless rolling. It is recommended that
you do not stop here. In this section the canal is about 70' higher than the north bank
countryside. The canal was cut out of the hillside and looks down on the countryside as
you face north looking towards Lake Ontario. You may hear VHF Radio calls like
"Seaway Sodus" along this stretch. This is a control station on Lake Ontario and has
nothing to do with the canal. It is just that you are close enough and uphill with a clear
line of vision to Lake Ontario at this point, such that you can sometimes receive VHF
radio signals here.

Mile 252.72, **Bridge E-136, Mitchell Rd** (16.18')

Mile 263.23, **Bridge E-137, State St** (16.10')

Mile 253.43, **Pittsford, Free Dock.** Tie up east of
Main St. Bridge (E-138) on south wall. Three
power stands, 2 with 15A and 30A service,
one with 30/50A. No cleats, only widely
spaced bollards. To the east of this wall is a
180' floating dock with three power stands
and 15/30A service. This dock has cleats.
Long concrete wall on north side but no
services. Town is on south side. Gift shops,
restaurant, and convenience store on north
bank. South on main to library, ATM and
pharmacy. West on Route 31 for 1.5 miles to
major mall with Wegman's Supermarket and
Eckerd Drugs. Free pump out west of E-139
bridge in front of DPW garage.

Canal harbor at Pittsford
Photo courtesy Tug44.org

Mile 253.50, **Bridge E-138, Main St** (16.10')

Mile 253.68, **Bridge E-139, railroad** (15.94')

Mile 253.91, **Bridge E-140, Monroe Ave** (21.10')

Mile 255.07, **Bridge E-141, Clover St** (20.00')

Mile 255.14, **Lock E32, Pittsford** (25')(RC), **Free Dock.** Tie up west of lock on south wall. Free pump out on the wall west of lock. Canal Park is suitable for small boats only. The lock doors on the upper side leak so that a waterfall occurs below the upper doors.

Lock 32 – Pittsford
Photo courtesy Tug44.org

Mile 256.36, **Bridge E-142, Edgewood Ave** (17.50')

Mile 256.40, **Lock E33, Henrietta** (25')(RC), **Free Dock.** Inside lock walls have been refaced. Tie up east or west of lock on south wall. Both walls are short. Note the spillway below the lock on the south side.

Mile 257.00, **Bridge E-143, Winton Rd** (21.35')

Mile 258.03 – 258.09, **Bridges E-144, Clinton Ave** (16.58') and **E-144A, I-390** (22.89')

Mile 258.14 – 259.88, **Bridges E-144B, I-390** through **E-146A, Kendrick Rd,** lowest clearance 20.10'

Mile 259.95, **East Guard Lock**

Mile 260.02 – 260.40, **Bridges E-147, railroad** through **E151, pedestrian**. Lowest clearance is 17.4'.

Mile 260.55, **Caution.** The Genesee River current can be swift as you cross it following the Erie Canal. Be sure to allow for this northbound current as you cross the river. Shoaling is a constant problem here and the Canal Corporation dredges on a regular basis. Divert north on the scenic Genesee River 2 miles to Rochester. The floating docks at Corn Hill Landing on west side of river reportedly have depths that are less than 3'. Call the dockmaster (585-325-7116) for details. Another option is to tie along the wall in front of the restaurant as far north as possible. **Free Dock**. No overnight docking. Convenience store nearby. Many restaurants and stores within ½ mile walk north. Walk a half mile north and see the Rochester aqueduct and library, a beautiful gorge and falls. Rochester celebrates the Corn Hill Arts Festival in mid-July with many tents displaying artist works and stands selling food.

.   **Historical Note.** As the Erie Canal proved to be very successful, other canals were constructed to tie into the Erie Canal. One such canal was the Genesee Valley Canal that joined the Erie Canal near here. The Genesee Valley Canal connected Rochester with Olean, NY and generally followed the Genesee River south. Today, as with most canals in the United States, it has been abandoned. Traces of the canal can be seen if one drives along the Genesee River, but it is no longer navigable south of the present Erie Canal junction.

Rochester Skyline
Photo courtesy Don Robertson, M/V Cygnus

A long aqueduct (800') once spanned the Genesee River in Rochester. Its replacement built in 1842 is now the base of the Broad Street Bridge in Rochester.

Mile 260 to 264, **Historical Note.** This section of the canal, often referred to as the "Rock Cut", required some of the most extensive excavation of the entire canal. The deep cut was made through solid rock and as you proceed through it you can imagine how hard it must have been to make this cut 80 years ago, before modern earth moving machinery.

Mile 261.02, **West Guard Lock**

Mile 261.26 – 265.94, **Bridges E-160, railroad** through **E-170, Long Pond Rd.** Lowest clearance 17'.

Mile 26.47, **Historical Note.** The original Erie Canal used to go directly into downtown Rochester. The original canal and lock entrance can be seen on the north bank opposite.

Mile 267.45, **Allen's Canalside Marina,** (716-426-5400, G) Travel lift.

Mile 267.59, **Henpeck Park, Free Dock.** Tie up to north bank at 100' park wall. No services.

Mile 267.64, **Bridge E-171, Elmgrove Rd** (16.98')

Mile 267.95, **Greece Canal Park. Free Dock.** Park, no overnight stay allowed.

Mile 268.75, **Bridge E-172, Manitou Rd** (21.82')

Mile 269.83, **Bridge E-173, Gillett Rd** (16.97')

Mile 269.93, **Spencerport Guard Gate**

Mile 271.20, **Spencerport, Free Dock.** Tie up east of the **lift Bridge E-174** (17' open) on the old terminal 1000' north wall. Three power stands with each having two 30A and 4 15A outlets. Small park with gazebo and drinking fountain/water hookup. Watch the depth. Posted with 48 hour limit. East of the bridge on the south wall is a new 500' dock with four power stands with two 30A and 4 15A outlets and water hookup. Restrooms showers, a small museum and library with WiFi is in the Spencerport Depot and Canal Museum. Tie up west of the lift bridge on south wall at the 200' wooden face dock with gazebo and 3 electric pedestals. Each pedestal has 4 30A outlets and two water spigots. West of the lift bridge on the north there is a free pump out on the 50' dock (no overnight).

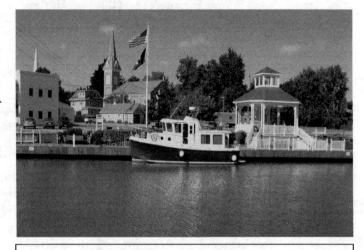

Free dock in Spencerport
Photo courtesy Tug44.org

In Spencerport you will find the Village Plaza shopping center. The Taste of Texas Bar-B-Q is reportedly quite good. Post Office ½ block south, zip is **14559.** Free concerts on Sunday night during the summer. A new Tops Supermarket is one block south.

Historical Note. Spencerport celebrates Canal Days each year in late July. Featured are live entertainment, a fishing contest, parades, pony rides, and a one-mile tube craft race on the Erie Canal.

Mile 270.28 to 274.21, **Roaming Operator.** A single operator works both the E-174 Union Street Lift Bridge (LB) and the E-178 Washington LB.

Miles 271.47 – 272.49, **Bridges E-175, Martha St** (16.97') **and E-176, Trimmer Rd** (16.98')

Mile 273.3, **Adams Basin LB, Free Dock.** Tie up east of lift bridge on south town wall**.**

Miles 274.21 to 278.76, **Bridges E-178**(lift) **to E-181 Park Ave** (lift), low clearance 16.98'.

Mile 278.76 and 278.93, **Roaming Operator.** The same individual operates both the E-181 Park Ave. LB and the E-182 Main St. LB.

Mile 278.85, **Brockport.** Visitor center located on the south wall between lift bridges and houses restrooms, showers, laundry. Power, water and WiFi available. South wall has 10 power stands, each with 15/30A service. Pump out is west of lift bridge on north side. Watch your superstructure. In January 2021 dockage was $15 for vessels 40' and longer.

Fazools Italian Restaurant is at east end of south wall just before the bridge. They offer free ice to boaters. The Stoneyard Bar and Grill is located at the opposite end of the south wall just east of the North Main Street LB. Thursday night concerts. The State University of New York (SUNY – Brockport) is located in this community and as a result this is very much a college town.

Visitor Center at Brockport
Photo courtesy Tug44.org

South of canal restaurants, antique shops, laundromat, pizzeria, candy store, Post Office (1/2 block south of lift bridge), ATM, bookstore, and more. Just over one mile south on Main Street is a large mall with Wegman's Supermarket, fast food, liquor store, restaurant, small strip mall, fast food restaurants, etc. Wal-Mart, which previously was located in this mall, has relocated and is now about 3 miles away.

North of canal 1 block Auto Parts, pizza restaurant, Dollar General. Two blocks north Rite Aid Pharmacy, Pizza Hut, BBQ and ATM.

Historical Note. Cyrus McCormick established a factory in Brockport in what is now the McCormick Park, near the Park Street Bridge. Here the first 100 wheat reapers in the world were built starting around 1874.

Mile 279.21, **Bridge E-183, Smith** (16.84')

Mile 279.80, **Brockport Guard Gate, Free Dock.** On the south bank, east of guard gate, tie up to short wall. Park with no services.

Mile 280.47, **Bridge E-184, Redmond Rd** (16.95')

Mile 282.03, **Bridge E-185, State Route 31** (17.04')

Mile 283.00, **Bridge E-186, Bennetts Corners** (16.89')

Mile 283.43, **Holley Canal Park, Free Dock.** Tie up east of East Avenue lift bridge on the

wooden face dock on the south wall in front of the park. Water and seven 30A (single outlet) stands. Pump-out at west end of dock. Showers, rest room, pond with fountain, and picnic tables. Get the combination from Lift Bridge operator. Or, tie up west of the bridge on south wall with no service. Small town setting with Sav-A-Lot Supermarket, bank, pizza store, Laundromat, library (with internet) and a small farmer's market. All of this is about 5 blocks SW from the dock. There is an excellent map of the village at the dock.

Take the shortcut to town. From the gazebo at the dock, follow a paved path downhill thru the town park, picnic area, and pond with fountain. After the park you will see a small railroad museum. If instead, you turn left before the railroad museum on the gravel road you will find a wonderful surprise. The gravel road leads to a little hollow with a nicely landscaped second town park with picnic shelter. At this park is a beautiful waterfall that may make this one of the prettiest stops on the Erie Canal. (See photo on the previous page.)

Visit the restored 1907 railroad depot, now a museum. Concerts in the summer at park with waterfall. New skate park for kids. Post Office zip is **14470.**

Town dock and park at Holley

Mile 283.48, **Bridge E-187, East Ave LB** (16.76') when open. **Roaming Operator.** The same individual operates both this bridge and the Hulberton Road LB at mile 286.58.

Mile 284.14, **Bridge E-188, North Main St** (16.76')

Mile 284.16, **Holley Guard Gate** (17')

Miles 285.00 – 285.48, **Bridges E-189, Telegraph Rd** (16.83') and **E-190, Groth Rd** (16.82')

Mile 286.58, **Bridge E-191, Hulberton LB** (16.76' open), **Free Dock.** Tie up east or west of LB on north wall. Park with picnic tables west of LB.

Mile 287.89, **Bridge E-192, Fancher Rd** (16.34')

Mile 288.65, **Bridge E-193, Hindsburg** (16.66'), **Free Dock**. Tie up west of the bridge on the north wall. Room for two boats. Very isolated.

Miles 287.89 – 292.37, **Bridges E-194 through E-198**, minimum clearance 16.64'.

Mile 292.98, **Bridge E-199, Ingersoll LB** (16.59') when open. First LB as you come into Albion from the east.

Mile 292.98 to 296.41, **Roaming Operator.** Both the LB's in Albion and the Eagle Harbor LB are operated by the same individual.

Mile 293.06, **Albion Canal Park, Free Dock.** Tie up between bridges E-199 and E-200 on either north or south walls. Preferred dockage would be east of LB on south wall. Eleven electric stands with two 30A outlets on each on south wall east of Main St. LB. Six water standpipes. Restrooms and shower facilities. Lift bridge operator has the four-digit code for these facilities.

West of the bridge are long unimproved walls north and south that provide dockage but no services. Limited restaurants and shops near the canal. The American Legion Post next to the Laundromat has a fish-fry on Friday, Steak Roast on Saturday. Family Dollar Store, pharmacy and Burger King 0.4 miles south. Rite Aid Drugstore, ATM, restaurants, etc. on corner of East and Main. PO is 3 blocks south, zip code **14411**. Ice ½ block north at convenience store.

Walk south to RT 31 and then west a total of 1.1 miles for TOPS and Save-A-Lot supermarkets. Farmers Market on Saturday in the Save-A-Lot parking lot.

Historical Note. Albion sponsors a Strawberry Festival each year in early June. The highlights include a Friday evening strawberry social, strawberry specialties, and a Saturday strawberry pancake brunch.

Albion is the home of George Pullman. He invented the railroad sleeping car named after him. It is thought that when he lived and worked in Albion from 1848 to 1855 he got the idea from seeing the canal boats.

Note the silver dome on the 1858 Greek Revival Country Courthouse. Take a walking tour of this quaint town with its many homes and churches on the National Register.

Village of Albion docks
Photo courtesy Tug44.org

Mile 293.15, **Bridge E-200 N Main St LB** (16.57') when open.

Mile 294.26, **Bridge E-201, Lattins Farm** (16.59')

Mike 294.29, **Albion Guard Gate** (16.65')

Mile 296.41, **Bridge E-203 Eagle Harbor LB** (16.58') when open. Tie up ½ mile east of LB on either north or south canal walls. Tie up west of the lift bridge on north bridge wall. Rural bedroom community with no services. There is a small fee for staying here.

Mile 297.94, **Anchorage.** Vessels can anchor in the basin on the south side of the canal in 8-10' about half way in this basin. Water is shallow further in.

Mile 299.47, **Bridge E-206, Knowlesville LB** (16.57') when open, **Free Dock.** Tie up west of Knowlesville LB on either north or south bridge walls.

Mile 299.47 to 304.13, **Roaming Operator.** The same individual operates the Knowlesville LB and Prospect St. LB in Medina.

Mile 301.07, **Historical Note.** The Erie Canal crosses over Culvert Road on an aqueduct. This is the only place where you can drive under the Erie Canal.

S/V Manatee crossing over Culvert Road
Photo Courtesy Jeff Bacon

Mile 301.84, **Bridge E-207, Beals Rd** (16.51')

Mile 302.64, **Bridge E-208, Bates Rd** (16.50')

Mile 302.65, **Medina Guard Gate, Free Dock.** Tie up to north bank on short wall west of the gate. Isolated boat launch.

Mile 302.79, **Medina Terminal Wall & Park, Free Dock.** Tie up to very long terminal wall on north bank. No cleats. Isolated. No services.

Mile 303.45, **Bridge E-209, Pleasant St** (16.71')

Mile 303.47, **State Street Park, Free Dock.** West of the Pleasant St. fixed bridge, tie up to north wall. No cleats. No services, isolated.

Mile 303.51, **Historical Note.** The Erie Canal crosses over the Orchard Creek aqueduct just west of the Pleasant St. fixed bridge.

Mile 303.65, **Canal Port Medina, Free Dock**. Tie up east of Eagle St. fixed bridge on north or south town walls. Looking from the east, the south wall is approx. 280 feet with water and five 30A electric stands. There is another 135 feet of newly refurbished all with cleats but no services. Finally there is another 400 feet of old concrete with ring cleats and no services. Free pump out. Restrooms and showers in Canal Marine Park. Lift bridge operator has the five-digit code for these facilities.

Medina terminal wall

No services on the north wall. This wall sits about 100' above the landscape below. There is a river and waterfall north of and below the north wall.

Free pump out west end of dock just before fixed bridge. (Disguised as an out house complete with crescent moon) Water is at a spigot between the pilings along the town dock. Look, it is there.

On Center Street find Medicine Shoppe Drug Store, gift shop and Laundromat. South on Main Street find Radio Shack, Chinese restaurant, restaurants, and liquor store. ½ mile south on main is a mini mart. 1 mile south at the intersection of route 31 is a propane fill, ice cream store, and Subway Shop. Several cruisers have reported that Zambistro's Restaurant is excellent. Regional transit has an all-day pass and senior fares.

There is a very impressive railroad museum in Medina in the large original rail freight depot building, which boasts a 192' by 14' HO-scale model train setup. Music by the Canal Friday nights June to August.

Historical Note. For more than 80 years sandstone was quarried in Medina. Medina Sandstone was used in important buildings all over the United States and was even exported to Cuba and England. Today as you walk around Medina, note the number of buildings that use Medina Sandstone.

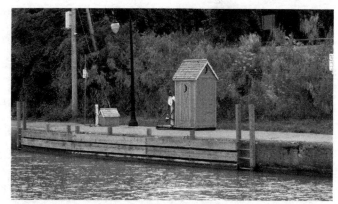

Pump Out at Medina
Photo courtesy Tug44.org

Mile 303.88, **Bridge E-210, Eagle Street** (16.70')

Mile 303.94, **Medina, Free Dock.** East of Prospect St. LB tie up to long walls either north or south of canal. Picnic tables on north side in Lions Park. No services.

Mile 304.13, **Bridge E-211, Prospect St. LB** (16.56') when open. West bound, the bridge is around a blind corner in Medina. Call ahead to make sure the roving operator will be there to open for you.

Mile 305.63, **Bridge E-212, Marshall Rd** (16.48')

Mile 307.34, **Middleport Guard Gate** (16.30')

Mile 308.87, **Bridge E-216, Main Street LB** (16.68') when open.

Mile 308.99, **Middleport Park, Free Dock.** Tie up west of Main Street LB on north or south bridge walls. 120' of the wall west of bridge on the south side was refurbished in 2005. Restroom/shower facility at the back of the police station. 30A/15A electric available on north and south wall west of lift bridge. Twelve 30A stands on south wall and six 30A stands on north wall. Free pump out west of bridge on north wall. (Bridge tender has the key.)

Village of Middleport docks.
Photo courtesy Tug44.org

You also can tie up east of the lift bridge on north wall. Five electric stands with 2 30A and 1 20A each.

Bank with ATM, Post Office, Village Pizza, Pony's Irish Pub, Portside Café all within a few blocks. Dollar General and 7-11 approximately one mile.

Mile 308.87 to 313.75, **Roaming Operator.** The same individual operates both the Middleport Main Street LB and the Gasport LB.

Mile 309.59, **Bridge E-217, Carmen Rd** (16.56')

Mile 310.40, **Bridge E-218, Peet Street** (16.56')

Mile 311.95, **Bridge E-219, Wruck Rd** (16.62')

Mile 312.54, **Bridge E-220, Slayton St** (16.76')

Mile 313.22, **Gasport Marina,** (716-772-2964). On the south bank.

Mile 313.75, **Gasport Guard Gate.** (16.65')

Mile 314.15, **Bridge E-222, Gasport LB** (16.65') when open.

Mile 314.19, **Gasport Landing, Free Dock.** Tie up west of lift bridge on 250' south wall at Gasport Lions Memorial Park. Three 30A stands. Road noise from traffic on lift bridge. Pizzeria and Canal Side Inn, Ace Hardware, restaurant, and laundromat.

Miles 315.21 – 318.92, **Bridges E-223, Orangeport, E-224, N Canal Rd, E-225, Day Rd, E-226, Cold Springs.** Minimum clearance 16.62'.

Mile 319.05, **Nelson C Goehle Public Marina,** (716-439-6624). Cash only. Park adjacent with Widewaters Drive-In Café across the street.

Mile 319.50, **Bridge E-228, Lake Ave** (16.61')

Mile 319.92, **Bridge E-229**, **Lockport Adams Street LB** (16.67'). No longer operational and in raised position.

Mile 320.11, **Bridge E-230, Lockport Exchange St. LB** (16.67') when open. **Free Dock.** Tie up east of lift bridge on south wall (250'), no services.

Mile 320.43, **Bridge E-231 railroad** (48.00')

Mile 320.65, **Lock E34, Lockport** (25')(C) The south chamber wall is in much better condition than the north.

Mile 320.67, **Bridge E-232, Pine Street** (44.51')

Two new locks at Lockport on the left and five old locks on the right.

Mile 320.72, **Lock E35, Lockport** (24')(C), **Free Dock.** You cannot stop between lock 34 and 35 because it is a staircase lock and there is no "between". There is space for 2 40' vessels to tie up west of Lock 35 behind the north lock wall. Turn 180° to starboard and proceed down the narrow channel which is marked with white buoys on your port. Tie off to starboard. When departing this area you will have to back out. If you are the forward most vessel and someone is tied up to your stern, they will have to move first. Somewhat isolated but an easy walk to town for shopping. Restaurants within 2 blocks, movie and library 3 blocks east on south bank.

During the summer you can take the Lockport Cave & Underground Boat Ride. This tour is of an old 1600' water tunnel that used to supply a power plant.

Historical Note. Originally there were two sets of five step locks at Lockport. This allowed boats to go both east and west at the same time. Today, two modern locks have replaced the southern 5 locks. The original northern five locks are still in place, but now used for overflow. There is a small Erie Canal museum at lock 34 (Walk from lock 35).

Mile 320.82, **Bridge E-233, Main St** (21.20')

Mile 320.97, **Bridge E-234, Transit Rd** (25.70')

Mile 321.15, **Lockport, Free Dock.** Tie up ½ mile west of lock 35 on long north canal wall. Isolated.

Miles 321.25 – 323.79, **Bridges E-235, Prospect St, E-235A, pipeline, E-236A, Summit Ave., E-237, Robinson Rd.** Minimum clearance 21.90'.

Mile 325.09. **Pendleton Guard Gate** (20.62').

Mile 325.31, **Bridge E-238A, Fisk-Fiegle** (25.00')

Mile 327.34, **Bridge E-240, Tonawanda Creek Road** (25.33')

Mile 327.41, **Ship and Shore Restaurant.** On the south bank of the canal, this restaurant provides dockage while dining. Located just west of bridge E-240. In the fall of 2014 it was reported this dock was in poor condition with only 3' of depth. Room for one boat. In small inlet, not on canal.

Mile 329.96, **Bridge E-241A, Campbell** (25.13')

Mile 330.06, **Amherst Marine Center, (**716-691-6707, G). On the south bank just west of bridge E-241A.

Mile 330.10, **Private Dock.** Caretaker, who lives on site, will allow transient docking. Six 30A electric stands and water.

Mile 331.44, **Bridge E-242, Bear Ridge Road** (25.01')

Mile 333.36, **West Canal Park and Marina.** North side, **Free Dock.** 100' on each side of ramp.

Mile 333.62, **Bridge E-242A, Niagara Falls, US 62** (22.32')

Mile 334.96, **Bridge E-243A, Robinson** (24.00')

Mile 337.55-57, **Bridges E-244A and E-244B, SR 425** (20.00')

Mile 338.14, **Bridge E-246, railroad** (20.05')

Mile 338.20, **Tonawanda.** This stop is usually busy even though this is the largest docking facility on the canal. During the summer the wall fills up early. Free summer concerts Wed, Fri and Sat June to August. Concerts can be loud and run late. There is a bike trail starting here that runs 100 miles to Palmyra, NY.

For all intents, all docking is between the railroad bridge on the east and the Webster Street bridge on the west. Between these bridges docking will be either east or west of the Delaware Street bridge. The south wall east of the Delaware Street bridge has plenty of depth with water and 30A electric. Be aware that this wall is high and it may be difficult for some to get on and off the boat. The north wall east of the Delaware Street bridge has about 10 foot depths. Water and 30A electric are only available east of the Dockside Inn. West of the Delaware Street bridge on the south side is a low wall with water and 30/A electric. There is room

Gateway Harbor at Tonawanda

for 4 or 5 boats but the water is reported to be as low as 4 feet. Across on the north side there is dockage with water and 30/A electric with depths around 5 feet. Overnight charge January 2021 $30/night for vessels 40' or less, $35/ night over 40' included electric. North and south wall have their own dockmaster. Dockmaster's office on south side has coin laundry, restrooms, and showers. Public rest rooms on north wall close to Main Street Bridge. Immigration phone on north wall adjacent to Delaware Street bridge. On Delaware Street south of canal find Burger King and Walgreens Drug Store.

On River Road south side of the canal find McDonalds, fast food, restaurants, shopping, Tim Horton Donuts Shop, Hollywood Video, large Tops Supermarket, and good public transportation to malls and other shopping. Bus in front of McDonalds also goes to Niagara Falls if interested. Canal Fest celebrated in mid-July. The Herschell Carousel Factory Museum is in North Tonawanda. Finally, this is an excellent place to leave your vessel for the day and visit Niagara Falls; a 20- minute ride using Uber/Lyft.

Mile 338.31, **Bridge E-247, Delaware St** (19.21')

Mile 338.44, **Bridge E-248, Webster St** (20.00')

Mile 338.54, **Bridge E-249, SR265** (24.00')

Mile 338.58, **Wardell Boat Yard, (**716-692-9428 G,D,P). On the north bank west of bridge E-249. Steps and unsteps masts. Call before stopping to make certain fuel is available.

Mile 338.74, **End of Canal.** The Erie Canal ends where it enters the Niagara River. Boaters wishing to visit Buffalo can do so by traveling south on the Niagara River some 10 miles through the Black Rock Lock to Buffalo Harbor. Expect a very strong current, which can be as high as 3 mph until reaching the lock. Call the lock on VHF 16 or 716-879-4403.

Chapter 5

The Oswego Canal

As the Erie Canal began to prosper, the people living along the Oswego River became concerned, lest they be left out of this new economical means of transportation. Just as the Erie Canal was completed in 1825, the state of New York authorized the money necessary to build the Oswego Canal some 38 miles from Syracuse on the Erie Canal to Oswego on Lake Ontario. Construction started in 1826 and opened for traffic in 1828.

Like the Erie Canal, the Oswego Canal was originally only 4 feet deep and had 18 locks. The canal was actually a ditch dug alongside the Oswego River and Lake Onondoga which carried barge traffic pulled by mules or horses. Over the years, the Oswego Canal was dredged to a depth of 10 feet. But, around the turn of the century, just as with the Erie Canal, it became obvious that a wider and deeper canal was needed. Since much of the traffic was now self-propelled, it was no longer necessary to use a ditch with a towpath, but rather the new canal could use the wider and deeper riverbed. The new wider and deeper canal with a controlled depth of 12 feet was opened in 1917. The Oswego Canal became shorter by virtue of the fact that the Erie Canal now passed north of Syracuse through Lake Oneida, cutting nearly 14 miles off the original Oswego Canal.

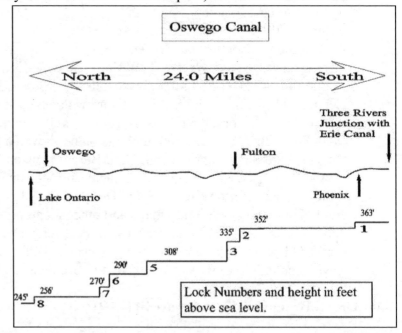

Today the Oswego Canal has a controlled depth of 14' and a controlled height of 20'. It is 24 miles long and has 7 locks. The locks are numbered 1 to 8 with no lock number 4. The original plans called for a lock 4, but as the system developed it was determined that a lock 4 was not needed and it was easier to leave all the other locks numbered as they were. As pointed out in other canal sections in this book, leaving a lock number out is not unique to the Oswego Canal. The Erie Canal has no lock 1 or 31 and the Champlain Canal has no lock 10.

From the Three Rivers Point (mile 160 of the Erie Canal) the Oswego Canal drops from 363 feet above sea level to 245' above sea level at Lake Ontario in 7 steps. In general, the locks are more modern and in better shape than the Erie Canal locks. The people and towns along the Oswego Canal encourage boaters and there are many places to stop and visit as you travel this waterway. Places to stop and highlights along the canal are listed at the end of this section.

The trip north on the Oswego Canal takes you through the communities of Phoenix and Fulton to the larger city of Oswego. Oswego is a good place to refit your vessel if headed across Lake Ontario as well as offering historical sites such as Fort Ontario.

The Oswego Canal locks support no less than 8 hydro plants. These plants generate between 1,400 and 10,000 kilowatts each, providing electricity for many New York families. As you head north, there are many places where you can tie up your vessel at no charge and enjoy the local history and supplies. In the harbor at Oswego, the waters can get a bit rough as many boats use this harbor every day. So, if the weather forecast is not good for crossing Lake Ontario, you might consider waiting at the stop listed for the south side of Lock 8, until the weather is right. You can still walk to Oswego from there and get your supplies, but not be subjected to all the boat wakes in the harbor.

Oswego Canal Highlights

Mile 0.0, **Three Rivers**. The Oswego Canal begins at the junction of the Oneida and Seneca Rivers that form the Oswego River. This is mile 160 on the Erie Canal, page 33 of this book.

> **Historical Note.** The junction of the Oneida and Seneca Rivers was a point easily identified since the early 1700s. The Indians used this area as a meeting place. During the Revolutionary and French and Indian wars this was a place selected for forces to rendezvous, prior to moving on in force.

Mile 0.75, large canal maintenance facility on western side.

Mile 1.27, **Historical Note.** On the east side of the river between R10 and R12 is Stowell Island. Stowell Island is also known as Treasure Island. Settled in the mid-1600s by Jesuits as a mission. The story goes that in 1658, the French and the Jesuits were fleeing the Indians near Onondaga Lake. They camped on Stowell Island and left behind cannon and gold to lighten their load. No gold has ever been found, but the locals refer to the island as Treasure Island to this day.

Mile 1.77, **Historical Note.** When northbound, just before you reach Phoenix you will see 4 concrete bridge abutments in the water to the west of the channel. These abutments used to support the trolley bridge on the line that went between Oswego and Syracuse.

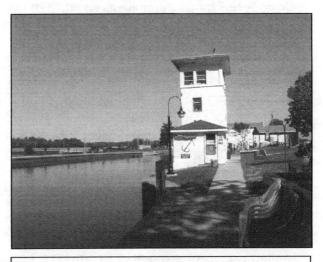

Mile 1.96, **Phoenix, Henley Park, Free Dock.** Tie up south of Lock O1 on the east wall near the white "Bridge House Museum" or on the wooden dock just south of the museum. Electric (15/30A), water, restrooms and showers are available. Bakery, café and other shops within two blocks. Groceries at a convenience store

The historic bridge house in Phoenix

and the Post Office (ZIP **13135**) are within four blocks. On the west wall you can tie off near the pavilion but there are no services. Phoenix is the home of the Bridge House Brats (www.bridgehousebrats.us), a volunteer youth group who, among other things, care

for the waterfront park and welcome visiting boaters. For tips they will deliver meals from local restaurants, escort you to local stores, and help carry provisions. Canal Days is celebrated in early June, and Independence Day fireworks the weekend before the 4th of July.

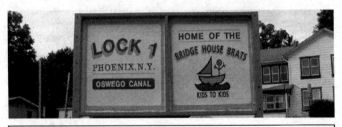

Photo courtesy Tug 44.org

Historical Note. Like so many of the old towns that were built almost entirely of wood, Phoenix burned in 1916. Phoenix had a vibrant manufacturing and retail business, when a fire started in a chair factory. All the manufacturing and retail businesses as well as many homes burned to the ground. The green bridge next to lock 1 survived the fire of 1916. Most other structures were lost. The retail district was rebuilt, but the manufacturing businesses never came back. The three story white bridge house adjacent to lock 1 was built in 1917 and housed the controls for an earlier lift bridge. Today you can visit this interesting mini museum and see many of the original controls that were used to operate the bridge, now gone.

Mile 2.15, **Lock O1, Phoenix** (10')(C&R), **Free Dock.** Tie up north of the lock and bridge on east wall.

Mile 2.19, **Phoenix LB** (7'), The only lift bridge on the Oswego Canal. Raises when lock opens.

Mile 5.27, **Bridge O-5, Hinsmansville** (24.89')

Mile 5.41, Old canal remnants on north shore.

Mile 7.75, Old canal remnants on east shore.

Mile 11.48, **Lock O2, Fulton** (18')(C), **Free Dock. Caution**: A fixed steel bridge with only 5' clearance spans the lock in the middle. Be sure to tie up south of this span if you require more than 5' clearance.
   Tie up south of lock on east wall or north of lock on west wall. The PO and a Rite Aid Pharmacy are located right next to Lock 2. Within two blocks is a Wendy's, Dunkin Donuts, Jreck Sub Shop and KFC. North between Lock 2 and 3 is the library on 1st Street.
   Fulton celebrates Canal Heritage Days in mid-July.

Mile 11.52, **Bridge O-8, Broadway** (39.90')

Mile 11.92, **Canal Landing Marina,** (315-599-4399). On east bank in basin. Free docking (up to 3 nights) with water and power. Easy access to town of Fulton. Short finger docks (max. boat length 42') and limited maneuvering space. Large vessels may block entrance. In July and August there are free concerts in the gazebo from 6:30-8:30pm.

Mile 12.06, **Lock O3, Fulton** (27') (C).

Mile 12.10, **Bridge O9, Oneida St** (28.20')

Mile 13.39, **Historical Note.** Pathfinder Island is located on the east side of the canal north of R94. This island was named after the lead character, Pathfinder, in James Fenimore Cooper's book of the same name. *"The Pathfinder"* centers on a trip taken down the Oswego River in 1759.

Mile 15.55, **Historical Note.** One of the original Oswego Canal locks is visible on the east bank behind day marker R106. It is currently used as a private slip.

Mile 15.62, **Historical Note.** As you go past G107 and G107A you pass Battle Island on the west. Battle Island is the site of a historic battle between the British and the French on July 3, 1756.

Mile 17.86, **Historical Note.** Old canal lock remnants visible on the east bank.

Mile 18.16, **Minetto, Free Dock.** 125' of floating dock on the west side, with three-30A power stands at a little park. Restrooms, picnic tables, mini-mart across street, phone, ATM, post office etc. Marilyn's Daily Dish Restaurant, and Stewart's Shops within walking distance, otherwise, limited shopping.

Mile 18.27, **Bridge O-10, Minetto Bridge Road** (24.40')

Floating dock at Minetto
Photo courtesy Tug44.org

Mile 18.49, **Lock O5, Minetto** (18')(R). No docking and no services. **Caution:** Watch for strong currents above and below this dam.

Mile 21.78, **Lock O6, Oswego** (20')(R&C). **Free Dock.** Tie up south of lock 6 on short east wall. No services.

Mile 22.45, **Lock O7, Oswego** (14')(P&R). **Free Dock.** Tie up north of lock 7 on east wall. Walk north into Oswego to visit historic Fort Ontario (11 blocks), grocery (west side 6 blocks), Laundromat (9 blocks) and many restaurants. The Post Office is on the west bank opposite lock 7, but is about a 0.9-mile walk. Paul's Big M Supermarket at corner on west bank.

Miles 22.48 – 22.73, **Bridges O-11** (21.67'), **O-12 Utica St** (35.07'), **O-13** (21.15')

Mile 22.89, **Lock O8, Oswego** (10')(C&R). **Free Dock.** Tie up south of lock on east wall. Be aware that close to the lock this wall is very rough and there are no cleats or rings to tie to; only bollards. Further south and closer to Lock 7 the wall flattens out and there are cleats. Very well protected and picnic tables. You can also tie up north of the lock in the harbor for a fee.

Park and dock area between Locks 7 & 8.
Photo courtesy Tug44.org

Mile 22.92, **Bridge O-14, Bridge St** (26.50')

Mile 23.00, **Alex's On the Water** (315-343-7700. Located at The Quality Inn and Suites, limited overnight docking is provided. Electric, water, restroom and showers.

There are three marinas in Oswego. Oswego Marina (315-342-0436 G,D,P) is on the east bank in a basin just past Alex's. After exiting the canal, in the large basin to the west is the International Marina (315-343-0688) and the Wright's Landing Marina (315-343-8430, P).

The east and west walls north of Lock 8 are operated by the Oswego Marina. It is $20 overnight without electric on the east wall. The west wall has 4 each 30A power pedestals and is still $20. Deposit payment in the box provided using the Dockage Permit form provided on the stand. There is also a 200' floating dock at the north end of the high east wall.

Courtesy docking is available on the east bank just before (south of) lock 8. You may find space in front of the high rise apartment building but often this area has commercial traffic tied to the wall. If so move further south toward the Utica Street Bridge. On East First Street opposite the pedestrian bridge is The Oswego Tea Company Café and Bakery. Tim Hortons and a convenience store are also on this street, just prior to the café. Beyond the café one block on East Oneida is the library.

Within 3 blocks north of Lock 8, restaurants, ATM, Eckerd Drug Store, and hardware store. West within 3 blocks, Paul's Big M Supermarket, movie theater complex, drug store, Dollar Store, ATM, restaurants, and gift shops. Four blocks south on west bank is the post office.

Each Thursday during the summer part of 1st Street (west side of lock) is closed for a large farmer's market. It is open from 5 to 9pm. Harborfest is held in the last week of

July. City bus stand just east of Bridge Street Bridge. Bus runs east about every 20 to 30 minutes 8am to 9pm.

Historical Note. 6 blocks north on east bank is the Fort Ontario State Historic Site. The first fort built at Oswego was "The Fort of the Six Nations" built by the British in 1755. This fort was destroyed by the French, rebuilt by the British, destroyed by the Americans, etc. Over the years the fort at Oswego went from a dirt and wood structure to the impressive stone fort standing on the site today. Last rebuilt in its present day form between 1839 and 1844, today the fort is open to the public as a valued historic landmark. Be sure to plan three to four hours of your time to see Fort Ontario.

Fort Ontario in Oswego, NY

Historical Note. On the west side of the Oswego Harbor, north of the large white cement silos, is the H. Lee White Marine Museum. This museum displays the history of Oswego Harbor and Lake Ontario. Part of the museum is located in the Derrick Boat.

Mile 23.68, **End of Canal**. Green Can "1" marks the end of the Oswego Canal

Chapter 6

The Cayuga-Seneca Canal

The original Cayuga-Seneca Canal was only 4 feet deep and followed a path just to the east of the present day canal. Around the turn of the century when the Erie Canal was enlarged to provide 12' depth, the Cayuga-Seneca Canal was constructed in its present location. The Cayuga-Seneca Canal is actually two short canals joining the Erie Canal with Cayuga and Seneca Lakes.

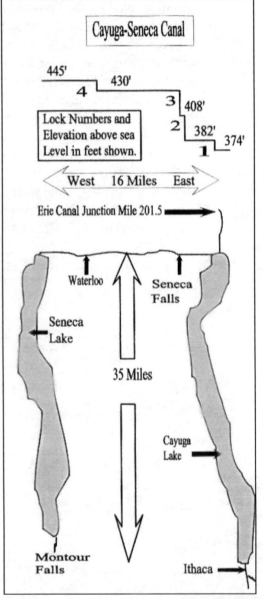

The waters are so clear in both lakes that you can easily see the bottom in 8'. Unfortunately, like Lake Champlain this allows weeds to grow profusely in any water less than 8'. Weeds become a problem later in the season, particularly when anchoring or cruising into shallow water.

From mile 201.5 on the Erie Canal, boaters travel south in nearly a straight line 3.9 miles to Lock 1 on the Cayuga-Seneca Canal. Vessels should have their clearance down to 16' if using the Cayuga-Seneca Canal. Once you leave the lock you must decide whether to continue on south into Cayuga Lake, or to proceed to the west on the Cayuga-Seneca Canal towards Seneca Lake.

Cayuga Lake is about 36 miles long and offers a lot for the cruiser. Clean water, state parks, yacht clubs and open water to anchor on. Cayuga Lake is deep at over 400 feet in some places. It is also long and skinny as befits one of the New York "Finger" Lakes. If you go all the way to the south end of Cayuga Lake, you will find a nice State Park operated marina on the outskirts of Ithaca. It is a good place to stay while you visit the sights in Ithaca.

Boaters who elect to proceed in the Cayuga-Seneca Canal follow a well-defined canal about 3 ½ miles to Lock 2 & 3. These staircase locks mark the entrance to Seneca Falls, a marvelous stop for cruisers. Once a prosperous mill town, today Seneca Falls is a sleepy little village that bears the distinction of being the birthplace of the Women's Rights movement.

Beyond Seneca Falls the Cayuga-Seneca Canal proceeds generally west past Waterloo, with its museum to Memorial Day, and Lock 4. West from Lock 4 about 5 miles you pass the Seneca Lake State Park Marina and enter Seneca Lake. This is the deepest Finger Lake at over 605 feet. Since you are about 445 feet above sea level at this point, part of Seneca Lake is actually more than 160 feet below sea level. On Seneca Lake fresh water fishing abounds and the surrounding countryside hosts many wineries. You can make arrangements to visit some of the wineries at the different marinas and yacht clubs.

At the south end of Seneca Lake, 34 miles from the Cayuga-Seneca Canal is Watkins Glen, famous for both auto racing and a unique natural gorge exposing much of nature's geological structure. Next to Watkins Glen at the south end of Seneca Lake is an extension of the Seneca Canal that takes you two and one half miles further south to Montour Falls.

The Cayuga-Seneca Canal opens up an area of cruising in the two Finger Lakes unique on the east Coast of the United States. History, culture, wineries, clean water, fishing and wonderful people abound. Be sure to allow one or two weeks for this area of the New York Canal System.

Caution – While the vertical clearance on the canal is 17.5' the railroad bridge on Cayuga Lake is 17.0'.

Cayuga-Seneca Canal Highlights

Mile 0.0, **Erie Canal Junction**. At mile 201.38 on the Erie Canal the Cayuga-Seneca Canal branches off to the south. See page 36 of this book.

Mile 0.54, **Bridge S-1A, NYS Thruway/I-90** (26.20')

Mile 2.97, **Bridge S-1, U.S. 20/SR 5 (Freebridge)** (21.60')

Mile 4.04, **Lock CS 1, Cayuga** (9')(R&C), **Free Dock.** Tie up either north or south of lock on east wall. There are no services but south wall has two power pedestals. Once on the south side of lock 1, you are at the same level as Cayuga Lake, 382' above sea level. **Note:** Be prepared for intersection to either Cayuga or Seneca Lakes 200 yards south.

Mile 4.21, **Cayuga Lake.** At marker R28 proceed south towards G33, keeping RG"CS" on your starboard, to enter Cayuga Lake. If you are proceeding to Seneca Lake, proceed west from R28 past R54 and follow the canal towards Seneca Lake. Cayuga Lake, some 35 miles long, offers fine cruising, many marinas, yacht clubs and several state parks. It also includes Ithaca with its college town atmosphere.

The channel to Cayuga Lake is long ending in markers R50 and G51. When returning from the south end of Cayuga Lake the coordinates for these last markers are N42º 51.55 and W76º 43.505.

Cayuga Lake

Stops on Cayuga Lake

Mile 4.63, **Lockview Marina,** (315-255-2936, G). On the east shore south of marker G33.

Mile 5.92, **Beacon Bay Marina,** (315-252-2849). On the east side just before bridge. Primarily a repair yard.

Mile 5.93, **Bridge S-2, railroad** (17.05')

Mile 9.27, Marker R50. Start of channel at north end. Coordinates N42º 52.57 and W76º 43.52.

Mile 10.32, **Trade-a-Yacht's Hibiscus Harbor Marina** (315-889-5086, G,D,P). On the east shore.

Mile 11.36, **Frontenac Harbor Marina,** (315-889-5532, G,D,P). On the east shore.

Mile 17.28, **Goose Watch Winery,** (315-549-2599). Docks on west shore at N42º 45.5 & W76º 46.2. Winery with tasting room just across road. Water depth at dock less than 5'.

Mile 17.78, **Aurora Town Dock.** On the east shore at approximately N42º 45.2 and W76º 47.3 is the exposed **Free dock** for Aurora, day use only. No services. Exposed anchorage adjacent. Picturesque 19th century town with restaurants, bar, food market, bakery, post office (**Zip 13026**), and hardware store. Tour MacKenzie-Childs Factory and Farmhouse.

Mile 33.65, Taughannock Point, N42º 32.87 and W76º 36.36. West side of lake anchor in 10-15' close to west bank. Protected from W to S winds. Dinghy to beach in cove or to the Taughannock Falls State Park just to the south. Nice spot in settled weather.

Mile 33.88, **Ithaca Yacht Club,** (607-272-9171, G). On the west shore 3 miles from the entrance to the Cayuga Inlet.

Mile 41.37, Entrance to Cayuga Inlet, R148. N42º 28.16 and W76º 31.46. **Note:** NY Canals website reported depths from here to the end of the harbor to be less than 10' in November 2017.

Mile 41.73, **Allan H Treman State Marina Park,** (607-273-3440). On the west side of the canal at the south end of Cayuga Lake. Will not accept reservations by phone or radio at this number. Reservation can be made through ReserveAmerica.com or by calling (800) 456-2267. Wegmans supermarket 1.8 miles from marina.

Mile 42.77, **Ithaca Boating Center/Cayuga Wooden Boatworks, Inc,** (607-272-1581). In the east branch of the canal at the end of Cayuga Lake, on the west bank. Boat Yard Grill next door.

Mile 42.80, **Historical Note.** Ithaca is the home of Cornell University and provides that unique flavor found only in a college town. A short walk from any of the marinas at the south end of Cayuga Lake will take you to Ithaca. Savor the laid-back college town atmosphere, visit the many bookstores, and take a walking tour of the university. Plan at least 4 hours for your walk and have lunch in town at one of the many restaurants. Post Office zip **14850.** In Ithaca, you can visit Cornell University (by bus), stop at the Cornell Art Museum, or visit the Farmers Market (Sat, Sun, Tue).

Cayuga Seneca Canal

Mile 5.00-6.00, **South Shore. Caution:** Low docks dot the southern landscape along this stretch and even a moderate wake will cause the owners to become upset. Go slow!

Mile 5.70, **Bridge S-3, State Route 89** (16.00').

Mile 5.99, **Bridge S-4, railroad** (17.30').

Mile 7.98, **Lock CS 2, Seneca Falls** (25')(C&R). No overnight stop here. **Note** - Locks 2&3 are "stair case locks" and as such when you enter one you must go through both.

Mile 8.04, **Lock CS 3, Seneca Falls** (25')(C&R). No overnight stop here. When you exit you are in Van Cleef Lake.

> **Historical Note.** Seneca Falls was once a thriving mill town that used the waterpower of the Seneca River to operate its mills. When the locks were built to provide a usable canal from Seneca Lake to Cayuga Lake, the river was dammed at the current location of locks 2 and 3. This created a 50' deep lake that submerged much of downtown Seneca Falls and the mills along the river.

Mile 8.65, **Bridge S-6, Ovid St** (16.85').

Mile 8.74, **Seneca Falls, Free Dock.** Tie up on the north town wall nearly 400' long. Seven 30A electric stands (each with two 30A outlets) and water along the wall. 200' floating docks at either end; however, they do not provide electric or water. The pump out ($1, 4 quarters) is at the east end of the floating dock, under the bridge. Bathroom, showers and a coin laundry are in the renovated canal museum. Register at the Community Center just

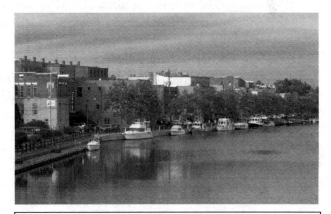

Terminal wall in Seneca Falls
Photo courtesy Tug 44.org

west of Bridge S-7 to receive a code for the restrooms. Available for use 6 a.m. to 7 p.m. The south wall next to the Seneca Knitting Mill has nine power pedestals with dual 30A service. Community garden is nearby. Maximum stay is 48 hours. Post Office zip is **13148.**

Seneca Falls offers a post office, restaurants, convenience stores, drug store, sock outlet, gift shops, etc. all within a mile on the north side. West on route 5 there are shopping centers some 2.5 to 3.5 miles away, one which hosts a Walmart.

New Wine Festival early May. Bass Derby celebrated mid-June. Canal Fest late in June. There is a Farmers Market every Wednesday in People's Park at the west end of the docks.

Historical Note. Seneca Falls is the birthplace of the Women's Right Movement. The obtaining of the right to vote, own property and many more rights started in this small village. Across the street from the Seneca Falls Terminal Wall is the Women's Rights National Historic Park.

Historical Note. The entire region around Cayuga and Seneca Lakes is famous for its winery's. You can rent a car in Seneca Falls to tour these wineries. Unfortunately, there are no wineries close enough to the water to be within an easy walk for a boater.

Mile 8.90, **Bridge S-7, Bridge St** (16.95')

Mile 9.16, **Bridge S-8, Rumsey St** (17.00')

Mile 10.85, **Bridge S-9, Mound Rd (River Rd Connector)** (17.65')

Mile 11.71, **Bridge S-10, Gorham St** (17.75')

Mile 12.26, **Bridge S-11, Washington St** (17.40')

Mile 12.31, **Lock CS4, Waterloo** (13')(R&C)**, Free Dock.** This final lock on the Cayuga-Seneca Canal raises your vessel to the height of Seneca Lake, 446 feet above sea level. Tie up east on the north or south wall. Also west of this lock on the north wall is Oak Island with a village dock and adjacent pavilion, BBQs and pump out. Three blocks north the town of Waterloo and liquor store, Chinese restaurant, Western Auto, and antique stores. Two blocks west of town center is a Save-A-Lot Supermarket. 1.5 miles east on route 5 is Walmart (approx.. ½ mile off Route 5), Tops Market, Aldi, Rite Aid and Kinney Drug Stores. Finger Lake Carp Derby celebrated early June.

Historical Note. Waterloo was the first community to celebrate Memorial Day. There is a museum in Waterloo to provide insight to this holiday.

Mile 12.34, **Guard Gate** (17.00')

Mile 13.93, **Hidden Harbor Marina,** (315-539-8034). On the north bank west of G109.

Mile 15.58, **Inland Harbor Marina,** (315-784-7255, G,). On the north bank by R122.

Mile 16.69, **Barrett Marine,** (315-789-6605, G,D,P). On south bank in basin is a large marina facility. Open-end travel lift.

Mile 16.91, **Bridge S-12, gas pipeline** (20.21')

Mile 16.95, **Bridge S-13, Lehigh Valley** (17.50')

Mile 17.00, **Bridge S-13A, SR 96A** (17.50')

Mile 17.02, **Bridge S-14, railroad** (17.30')

Mile 17.08, **Stivers Seneca Marine,** (315-789-5520, G,D,P). On the south bank just before the end of the Cayuga-Seneca Canal.

Mile 17.10, **Seneca Lake State Park Marina,** (315-789-2331, P). On the north bank just before the lake.

Mile 17.23, **Seneca Lake.** The canal structure as such ends here and you enter 34 mile long Seneca Lake with access to all the boating, fishing, and swimming it has to offer. Don't forget the towns of Geneva and Watkins Glen on this lake. Visit some of the marinas and yacht clubs and the two-mile long canal at the south end that takes you to Montour Falls.

Seneca Lake

Mile 17.49, R136. North end of lake at N42º 51.98 and W76º 56.68.

Mile 17.54, **Geneva Lakeshore Park, Free Dock.** Tie up at park on north shore of Seneca Lake. "Y" shaped floating docks protected by jetty just south of Ramada Inn (tan building with blue roof). Six slips on five finger docks, the largest being 35 feet. Others 25 feet. Three power stands offer 20A/30A service. Restroom and ice cream stand nearby as well as Chamber of Commerce center. Concerts weekly during the summer. Downtown Geneva has movies, post office, laundry, restaurants and drug store. Wi-Fi from Ramada works at dock. Wegmans Grocery Store is about one mile. Post Office zip **14456**

Mile 21.10, **Roys Marina,** (315-789-3094, G). On west shore.

Mile 29.70, **Historical Note.** On the western shore near Dresden is where the Crooked Lake Canal used to enter Seneca Lake. When in use, the Crooked Lake Canal connected Penn Yan (on Keuka Lake) with Dresden on Seneca Lake. The Canal, which was built starting in 1829, opened in 1833, and abandoned in 1877, had a total of 28 locks to drop 270 vertical feet in its 8 mile length. It followed the path of a natural stream, called the Keuka Lake Outlet through which Keuka Lake empties into Seneca Lake. Keuka Lake was formerly known as Crooked Lake. "Keuka" is a Seneca Indian word meaning "Lake with an elbow". Keuka Lake is unique among the Finger Lakes because it is Y-shaped rather than just being long and narrow.

Mile 24.00, **Sampson State Park Marina,** (315-585-6392). Electric is 125V/50A but the marina supplies adapters for 220V/50A or 120V/30A. Restrooms, showers a short walk, snack bar and gift shop a short walk.

Mile 51.41, **Watkins Glen. Village Marina,** (607-368-3466, P). Call for reservations. One-mile walk to center of town and pizzeria, bank, ATM, drug store, hardware store, antique shops, and video store, laundromat and several restaurants. Two blocks further is the waterfalls, She-Qua-Ga, or "tumbling waters". Walking trails take you from downtown Watkins Glen to the Watkins Glen State Park and the spectacular beauty of the gorge and waterfalls. Waterfront Festival mid-June. Post Office zip is **14891.**

Historical Note. Montour Falls was the terminus of the Chemung Canal that connected the southern end of Seneca Lake with Waverly on the Pennsylvania and New York border, some 30 miles to the south. A feeder canal half way to Waverly joined the Chemung Canal with Corning, NY to the west. Waverly, NY was at the head of the navigable Susquehanna River. Both these canals have been abandoned.

Montour Falls

Seneca Canal

The 2.5 mile long Seneca Canal joins Watkins Glen to Montour Falls and the terminus of the old Chemung Canal. This canal was dredged in 2000. 18' fixed bridge on this canal should not be a problem for vessels clearing 15' on the Cayuga-Seneca Canal.

Mile 51.85, **Glen Harbour Marina,** (607-535-2751, G,D,P). In canal at south end of Seneca Lake. First marina on east bank.

South Seneca Marina, (607-535-6690). In canal on west bank.

Frog Hollow Marina, (607-535-2671, G,P). In basin on west bank. ½ mile walk to Watkins Glen. Walmart 1 mile.

Chapter 7

Champlain Canal

The Champlain Canal should be called the "History Canal". Try to imagine! Before our country's independence, this waterway played an important role in our history. The British, French and Americans all traveled north and south along this stretch of country. Battles were fought, men died, and many were laid to rest along this path. Forts were built; most fell into disrepair with time. Forts Ticonderoga and Edward! The Battle of Saratoga! George Washington! Books like The New Erie Canal by John Fitzgerald educate, but only serve to whet your appetite. While cruising on the Champlain Canal it is impossible not to get drawn into the history of our country. At each stop you learn more and dig deeper. This is truly 60 miles of history. Listen… You can almost hear the men groaning as they drag the cannons from Fort Ticonderoga to Boston to attack the British.

In the late 1700s the most common route north from New York City to Canada was up the Hudson River to Fort Edward. Then by land, a portage to Lake George and on to Canada via Lake Champlain. All that changed in the early 1800s when the Champlain Canal was built. Completed in 1822 from Waterford to Whitehall on Lake Champlain, the Champlain Canal provided an all water route to Lake Champlain and points north.

As you travel north from the Erie Canal you follow the Hudson River about 37 miles until you reach Fort Edward. There, the navigable Hudson River ends and a man-made canal 23 miles long, connects the Hudson River with Lake Champlain. You begin at 15' above sea level, and steadily rise to 150' above sea level at mile 39 above Lock 8. Then after Lock 9 you descend to 97' above sea level at Lake Champlain. You will have to traverse a total of 11 locks numbered 1 to 12. Yes, we are missing a lock; we have no lock 10, as previously mentioned in other sections of this book. Once construction began, and a lock was eliminated, the other locks were not renumbered.

As with the other canals in the New York Canal System, the original Champlain Canal was very shallow and narrow when compared to today's canal. By 1916 the Champlain Canal had been dredged to its present depth of 12 feet with a controlled height of 17'. The busy commercial traffic of years gone by no longer exists. Today one sees almost no commercial vessels, but rather pleasure craft of all kinds. A trip up the Champlain Canal can be completed in one day or in several weeks. The 60 miles of the Champlain Canal provides much to interest the boater. Then the cruiser enters Lake Champlain, another large cruising area that also connects to the Richelieu Canal and all of Canada, the Great Lakes and the Saint Lawrence Seaway.

Controlling Height for the Champlain Canal

The vertical clearance of the Champlain Canal is 17'; despite what you may hear or be told. One railroad bridge, C5, between locks 3 and 4 is maintained at 15' 6" at most times. Prior to passing under this bridge call Lock 3 to determine the pool and clearance. The pool level above lock 3 is lowered to accommodate vessels up to 17'. Under abnormal river conditions (high rain fall upstream) vessels may be held at lock 3 or 4 while the pool level is allowed to drop. As an added safety precaution bridge height gages have been installed on both sides of bridge C5 to show the boater the air clearance of this bridge. Vessel operators are **cautioned** that if the C5 bridge height gages **do not** show sufficient clearance for their vessel they should **NOT try to pass under the bridge.** Instead contact the lock master at lock 3 and advise him of the situation.

Champlain Canal Highlights

Note: When cruising Lake Champlain and its tributaries you MUST physically disconnect your black water (sewage) overboard discharge and remove a section of hose. Failure to do so will result in a substantial fine if discovered by authorities.

Mile 025, **Junction – Erie Canal..** The Champlain Canal begins with marker G1 and R2 just north of the junction with the Erie Canal.

Mile 0.56, **Bridge C-2, 126th St** (19.93')

Mile 3.2, **Lock C1, Waterford** (14')(R&P)

Mile 3.80, **Lock One Marina,** (518-238-1321,G,D,P,WiFi). On the west bank in basin.

Mile 7.37, **Lock C2, Mechanicville** (18')(R&C)

Mile 9.29, **Mechanicville, Free Dock.** Tie up west side of river in front of the condominiums on 300' long wall. Eight 30A stands, pump out, water, showers and restrooms. During the summer the bugs under the street lamps can be unbelievable. They die and stick to your boat. Millions of them. They don't bite, but are a mess to clean up. Don't dock directly under the lamp posts and the bug problem is greatly reduced. Limited to a 3 day stay.

Depart dock on Terminal Street. Turn left one block to Post Office. Right on Main St., approximately ½ mile is Price Chopper and a Rite Aid Pharmacy. One block west going up Hill Street is Central Avenue with restaurants, Dollar Store, auto parts store, and other shops.

Town Dock – Mechanicville
Photo courtesy of Tug 44.org

Mile 9.42, **Bridge C-4A, State Route 67** (20.16')

Mile 9.92 **Lock C3, Mechanicville** (20')(R&P). No overnight stop. See text on Bridge C-5 below.

Mile 10.3, Bridge C-5, railroad. Caution: The NOAA charts show this bridge as 21'. That is the clearance at a normal pool 67.50. The pool is actually maintained above that at 73.50, which provides a clearance of only 15.5'. If you need additional clearance call Lock C3, 518-664-5171. Vertical clearance up to 21' can be achieved. If you are over 15' and approaching bridge C-5 from the north (Lock C4) or south (Lock C3), it would be a good idea to mention it to the appropriate lockmaster and make sure the pool is lowered for you.

Mile 11.76, **Lock C4, Stillwater** (16')(R&C). Short tie up wall north and south of lock on east wall. No overnight services. The town of Stillwater is on the west shore of the Hudson River and is a nice walk from the lock. Go north on lock access road 0.4 miles and turn west, crossing the canal and then the Hudson River. At the junction of Route 4/32 (0.5 miles) you will find a Stewarts Gas Station and convenience store. Continuing south on route 4/32 you pass Moreno's Pizza (0.6 mile), Frankie O's Pizza (0.7 mile), Pat's Subs and Pizzas and Don's Pizza (both 0.8 mile). Lots of pizza within 1 mile of lock. At mile 0.9 you come to Blockhouse Park in Stillwater, which is really the end of shopping in this area. Located in this park is the Stillwater Blockhouse, which is historically unique. It was built in part with timbers from Revolutionary era structures once standing within what is now Saratoga National Historical

Stillwater's Historic Blockhouse

Park, in Stillwater. It is a copy of a French & Indian War Stockade of the region, but was actually built in 1927 as New York State turned the site of the American Revolution's 1777 "Turning Point Battles" into an historical park. It is open to visitors from Wednesday to Sunday 12 noon to 4pm.

Historical Note. Fort Winslow was built in Stillwater in 1756. General Schuyler used the Dirk Swart house in Stillwater as his headquarters during the Revolutionary War. This house still stands today.

Mile 12.18, **Bridge C-6, County Rd 125** (27.16')

Mile 17.5, **Saratoga Battlefield.** Vessels can anchor east of channel south of R100 in 10' of water. Then dinghy across to west shore opposite marker R100. There is a large brown National Park sign at the water's edge. Keep in mind you are probably on private property. At the entrance to the Saratoga Battlefield National Park just west on Route 4 you will see the remains of the old Champlain Canal near the park sign. For those brave souls that like to walk, a 2.5 walk (mostly uphill) into the park gets you to the Visitors

Center and lets you visit this historical site. In addition, there is a 4-mile walking tour of the battlefield and a very interesting museum there.

Mile 25.00, **Schuyler Yacht Basin,** (518-695-3193, G,D,P,WiFi). Located west of island at G143.

Mile 25.13, **Bridge C-7, State Route 29** (27.06')

Mile 26.13, **Bridge C-8, Lock C5 Rd** (23.82')

Mile 26.17, **Lock C5, Northumberland** (19')(R&C), **Free Dock.** Tie up north of the lock at the 50' floating dock on the east side of the canal that is part of the Hudson Crossing Park. The park has over two miles of trails out to the dam plus a picnic pavilion with sculptures, mosaics and flower gardens. No services available. You can also tie up south of lock on the short west lock wall. This wall is about 4 feet above water and may make getting off the boat difficult. Tie alongside a ladder.

Exit canal park west one block and turn south on route 4/32. Lynn's Country Cafe 0.2 miles, Old Saratoga Café and Eatery 0.6 miles, traffic light 0.7 miles, Cumberland Farms Convenience Store and ATM 0.7 miles, General Schuyler's Pantry 0.8 miles, Stewarts Gas Station and convenience store 0.9 miles, 2nd traffic light 1.0 mile, Mac's Diner 1.1 miles, post office and Byron's Market and Grocery Store 1.1 mile. In addition to the above mentioned stores, there are some gift and knickknack shops along the route as well as the Second Hand Rose Thrift Shop.

Schuylerville Junction Lock

Visit the old Schuylerville Junction Lock near site of new lock. When the current Champlain Canal was built, it bypassed the Schuylerville terminal, so the Schuylerville Junction Lock was built around 1916 to provide continued access. The lock and terminal remained in use until the 1950s. A set of the original lock doors is also near the site.

On the west side of lock 5 you can see the remains of the old Champlain Canal.

Mile 27.42, **Bridge C-10, US Route 4** (19.70')

Mile 29.85, **Bridge C-11, Lock Rd** (21.95')

Mile 29.90, **Lock C6, Fort Miller** (16')(R&P), **Free Dock.** Tie up north or south of lock on east wall. High rough terminal walls. Widely spaced bollards for tie up. Quiet rural setting. Site of old Fort Miller.

Mile 30.26, **Bridge C-12, Fort Miller Rd**
(19.56')

Mile 31.01, **Bridge C-13, North River Rd**
(17.04')

Mile 31.84, **Crocker's Reef Guard Gate**
(19.10')

Mile 36.93, **Junction to Fort Edward, Free Dock.** As you approach lock 7 from the south, take the marked channel just to the west of the lock and parallel to it. Do not enter the larger Hudson River opposite R222! Follow the channel 0.8 miles as it curves to port and passes under a 19' railroad bridge and 26' highway bridge. Controlling depth 6'. The harbor was dredged in 2015. Just west of the two sets of bridges tie up to the 500' refaced town wall on the north side of the channel. 8 power stands with 30A electric and water. Post Office zip is **12828.**

Croker's Reef Guard Gate
Photo courtesy of Tug44.org

Terminal wall in Fort Edward.

Historic Fort Edward offers shops, restaurants, fast food, and hardware, all within 2 blocks. Go north from dock to the town main street (Route 4). Turn left (west) on Route 4 for Adrianna's Pizzas and Subs 1 block from the dock, Cumberland Farms Convenience Store and Gas Station (0.2 mile), Adirondacks Dollar Store (0.6 mile), ice cream parlor (1 mile), and then what used to be the main shopping area (1.1 miles) of Fort Edwards. In the shopping area is Agway Hardware, Pizza Hut, New China Restaurant, Subway, McDonalds and Dunkin Donuts. The Anvil Inn, 2 blocks south of the main harbor past the railroad bridge is reported to have excellent food. The Hannaford Supermarket is about 5 miles north on Route 4.

Bus service to Glens Falls and large mall. Bus departs from stand on Main Street of Fort Edward.

Fort Edward is also a good place to leave your boat while you run in to New York City by train.

Historical Note. Fort Edward was a key point in transportation up the Hudson Valley. It was in this area, before the canals, that boats were removed from the Hudson River and carried west towards Lake George, before continuing north.

Fort Edward was built at this location to defend and protect this waterway. Eventually, a feeder canal was built from Fort Edward to Glens Falls about 15 miles to the west. Today this canal is being cleaned up as a tourist attraction and a walking path exists along almost its entire length.

Starting in Fort Edward, an individual can walk or take a bike to Glens Falls following the old canal towpath. Only in Fort Edward has the canal been totally removed both where the railroad crossed the canal and on Canal Street. To find the Glens Falls

Feeder Canal and walking path, go east on East Street from the traffic light in the center of town near the boat docks. After four blocks (just before RR tracks) turn north on Wing Street. In four blocks a fitness trail joins the road at the intersection of Wing and Factory Streets. Take the trail into Mullen Park and follow it along the Old Champlain Canal. At Lock 1, turn left onto the paved segment of the trail. You can follow this trail for 7 miles to Glens Falls.

You will see several locks along the route, but at about 3 miles along you come to a series of 5 step locks ("The Five Combines") no longer in operation that clearly show how the locks were constructed then and how small they were. The historical display at the park at these step locks is most informative.

Series of 5 step locks called "The Five Combines" on the historic Glens Falls Feeder Canal. No longer used as locks, they nonetheless still serve as part of a water feeder canal for the Champlain Canal to this day.

Mile 37.03, **Lock C7, Fort Edward** (10')(R&P),

Mile 37.31, **Bridge C14, Broadway (SR4)** (17.43')

Mile 37.40, **Fort Edward (Secondary) Public Docks.** Depth is reportedly 6'. No services.

Mile 37.70, **Bridge C-16, Argyle St** (17.48')

Mile 38.37, **Bridge C-17, East St** (17.58')

Mile 39.21, **Lock C8, Fort Edward** (11')(R), **Free Dock.** Tie up north of lock on west wall. Quiet rural setting. Above lock is highest point above sea level on Champlain Canal. It is 1.8 miles from here back to the town of Fort Edward. Access road gate locked at night.

Mile 41.04, **Bridge C-18, State Route 196** (21.55')

Mile 43.45, **Bridge C-19, New Swamp Rd** (17.03')

Mile 45.04, **Lock C9, Smith's Basin** (16')(R&P), Tying at this facility is no longer allowed.

Mile 45.47, **Bridge C-21, State Route 149** (18.96')

Mile 47.73, **Bridge C-22, Baldwin Corners** (18.36')

Mile 49.37, **Bridge C-23, Clay Hill Rd** (18.98')

Mile 53.42, **Bridge C-25, State Route 22** (23.35')

Mile 54.28, **Lock C11, Comstock** (12')(R&P), **Free Dock.** Tie up north or south of lock on west wall. Quiet rural setting, but right next to a prison. (Food for thought)

Mile 55.51, **Bridge C-27, Ryder Rd** (18.88')

Mile 60.07, **Bridge C-28, railroad** (17.00')

Mile 60.19, **Bridge C-29, US Route 4** (18.65')

Mile 60.58, **Bridge C-30, Saunders St** (17.70')

Mile 60.58, **Lock C12, Whitehall** (15')(R&P). Uses **VHF-13;** operates 24-hours per day. When locking through lock 12, if you are southbound, you must tie to the east wall due to the way the lock floods. Northbound vessels may tie up on either side. **Free Dock.** Tie up south of bridge C30 on 600' west wall in town of Whitehall. Three 50/30/15A power stands. Showers and restrooms in the Community Center south of the mooring wall. A little further south there are two floating docks for small boats at the new pavilion.

Terminal wall at Whitehall.

You can also tie up south of bridge C-30 on east bank. Finally, there are 200' of floating docks north and south of bridge C-30 on the west bank.

Whitehall is the midpoint between New York City and Montreal. A bar, a few restaurants ("Historic Grounds" on Main Street is a must) and a Laundromat are in the downtown area. One must see is Skene Manor. Constructed in 1872-1874 and the home of former Supreme Court Justice Joseph H. Potter, it is on the National Historic Register. Whitehall celebrates the Whitehall Festival in mid-July. Farmers Market on Tuesdays during the summer 10am-3pm just south of Skenesborough Museum which is adjacent to west wall at bridge C30. Limited shopping (CVS, Putorti Market, hardware, Stewart's) within walking distance.

Amtrak also stops at Whitehall. Southbound to New York at 3:08pm and northbound from New York at 12:22pm.

Historical Note. Whitehall is known as the birthplace of the US Navy. Our first small navy of 12 vessels was constructed here in 1776. These vessels were used by Benedict Arnold to prevent the British from invading the colonies. The Skenesborough Museum in Whitehall provides an excellent display of the history of the defense of the Hudson Valley. If you go further north into Lake Champlain, you can learn more about the history of Benedict Arnold and his fleet at Vergennes, VT and Valcour Island.

Mile 60.87, **New Whitehall Marina at Lock 12**, (518-499-9700, G,D,P,WiFi). On the west bank just past the lock.

The Champlain Canal ends at Whitehall, but the adventure of cruising Lake Champlain lies just ahead. North of Lock 12 you enter Lake Champlain. At first it is a very narrow waterway, but soon opens into a large lake. Refer to Skipper Bob's Book *Cruising the Rideau and Richelieu Canals* for information on cruising Lake Champlain.

Skene Manor
Photo courtesy of Tug44.org

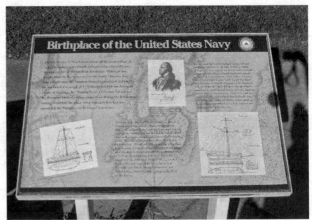

Photo courtesy of Glen & Jill Moore
m/v Last Dance

Cruising the New York Canal System

Appendix 1

2021 Fees and Hours of Operation

Pleasure craft fees for the 2021 navigation system have been waived.

The hours of operation for the 2021 season were not available at the time of production. The 2020 season is shown below for a general guide as to what to expect for 2021. Se the NY Canals website, www.canals.ny.gov for current information.

- **May 15 to October 14:** 7:00 a.m. to 5:00 p.m.

    In addition to the schedule listed above, the following locks and lift bridges will operate on demand from **7:00 a.m. to 10:00 p.m.** from **May 15 to September 16**:

- Lock C-1, Waterford
- Lock E-7, Vischer Ferry
- Lock E-8, Scotia
- Lock E-23, Brewerton
- Lock O-1, Phoenix
- Lock O-2, Fulton
- Lock O-3, Fulton
- Lock O-8, Oswego
- Lock E-24, Baldwinsville
- Main Street Lift Bridge, Fairport
- Lock E-32, Pittsford
- Lock E-33, Henrietta
- Spencerport Lift Bridge
- Adams Basin Lift Bridge
- Park Avenue Lift Bridge, Brockport
- Main Street Lift Bridge, Brockport
- Holley Lift Bridge
- Hulberton Lift Bridge
- Ingersoll Street Lift Bridge, Albion
- Main Street Lift Bridge, Albion
- Eagle Harbor Lift Bridge
- Knowlesville Lift Bridge
- Medina Lift Bridge
- Middleport Lift Bridge
- Gasport Lift Bridge
- Exchange Street Lift Bridge, Lockport
- Lock E-34/35, Lockport
- Lock CS-1, Cayuga
- Lock CS-2/3, Seneca Falls
- Lock CS-4, Waterloo

    In addition to the schedule listed above, the following locks and lift bridges will operate on demand from **7:00 a.m. to 7:00 p.m.** from **May 15 to September 16**:

- Lock E-25, May's Point
- Lock E-26, Clyde
- Lock E-27, Lyons
- Lock E-28A, Lyons
- Lock E-28B, Newark
- Lock E-29, Palmyra
- Lock E-30, Macedon

In addition to the structures listed above, Locks E-2 through E-6 and Guard Gate #2 in the Waterford Flight as well as Locks E-21 and E-22 will operate on demand from **7:00 a.m. to 10:00 p.m.** from **Thursday through Monday** from **May 15 to September 16.** During the same period, the hours of operation for the Waterford Flight will be **7:00 am to 6:00 p.m.** on **Tuesdays and Wednesdays**. Due to roving operators, some delays may be experienced during certain periods in the Waterford Flight.

Vessels arriving at the Waterford Flight from either direction prior to scheduled closing will be admitted through the entire Flight.

Vessels arriving at Lock CS-2/3 in Seneca Falls or Lock E-34/35 in Lockport from either direction prior to scheduled closing will be admitted through both chambers. Vessels arriving westbound at Lock E-21 in New London or arriving eastbound at Lock E-22 in Verona prior to scheduled closing will be admitted through both locks. Vessels arriving southbound at Lock C-4 in Stillwater or arriving northbound at Lock C-3 in Mechanicville prior to scheduled closing will be admitted through both locks. Vessels arriving at the Waterford Flight from either direction prior to scheduled closing will be admitted through the entire Flight.

Skipper Bob and First Mate Elaine

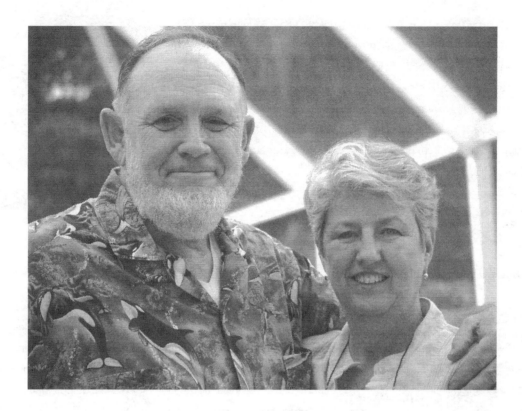

The late Skipper Bob and his wife Elaine cruised over 44,000 miles while living aboard both a trawler and a sailboat. They traveled up and down the Intracoastal Waterway several times, completed the Great Loop Route, explored the NY Canal System, the Trent-Severn, Rideau & Richelieu Canals, Georgian Bay and the North Channel. They cruised up the Ohio River to Pittsburgh and visited the National Park in the Dry Tortugas.

Elaine says; "Bob's purpose in writing the Skipper Bob guides was to make fellow cruisers adventures as comfortable and safe as possible. In authoring these guides, he wanted to provide others with the knowledge he gained through his years of experience. Added to that was sharing the years of experience and knowledge of other boaters that we met along the way. Bob's theory was "If you are going to be here you might as well pay attention". He took millions of notes and kept detailed logs. His guides were a part of him, not just something he wrote. Now they have become his legacy. I am very proud that they are continuing under the guidance of Waterway Guide."

The Skipper Bob Award

The Skipper Bob Award, first presented in 2008, was given at the AGLCA Rendezvous to individuals who made extraordinary efforts to assist the recreational boating community, just as Skipper Bob did during his life. The award was created by his widow, Elaine Reib, with the assistance of AGLCA members Ann and Bob Levine. Each recipient was given a signal flag from a set that Skipper Bob flew from his vessel. The award was retired in the Fall of 2014.

Fall 2014 – Fred Wehner

For many years Fred has assisted boaters on the New York waters, particularly the New York Canal System....providing free dockage at his residence, transportation from many locations, updates on canal status and projects, and more. He was a close friend of Skipper Bob, was instrumental in the initial publication of the canal guides, and continues to be a contributor. Fred was Elaine Reib's personal choice for the final Skipper Bob award.

Fall 2013 – Claiborne Young

Renowned speaker, author and founder of The Salty Southeast Cruisers' Net, in the words of Ron Stob, co-founder of AGLCA, "few authors and/or public speakers have left such a lasting impression on the boating public". Fred Myers states "I can attest to his deep and consistent commitment and dedication to recreational boating over the past 35 years". Great job Claiborne.

Fall 2012 - Bob Duthie

Bob has been personally responsible for the continued availability of Fred Myers' cruising guides to the rivers and lately Bob has done what the Corp of Engineers said they couldn't, reprint the river charts. Without the benefit of the charts and guides, cruising on the Tennessee, Cumberland Rivers and the Tenn-Tom would have been very hazardous. Congratulations Bob, you certainly have made it better for the rest of us.

Spring 2012 - Jack & Craig Dozier

As Publisher of Waterway Guide, Jack and Craig have been active supporters and sponsors of AGLCA since its founding in 1999. In addition, their purchase of Skipper Bob Publications has provided cruising boaters continued access to the renowned collection of cruising guides. Jack has made many presentations at rendezvous over the years.

Fall 2011 - Kelly Ezell

As marina manager at Joe Wheeler State Park, Kelly was a driving force behind the success of the first rendezvous there in the fall of 2004. Her task of preparing for 46 transient boats arriving at one time was complicated by a marina renovation project that was due to be completed just prior to loopers arrival. Her enthusiasm made it happen, not only that year, but for 5 more years. In 2009, Kelly was promoted to manager of the State Park lodge and marina complex and continues to make it happen for loopers.

Spring 2011 - Steve & Janice Kromer

Steve and Janice purchased AGLCA in 2007 and have led a very successful expansion of membership, events, sponsor participation, and most important, membership benefits. For current "loopers" and future "wanna bees", the semi annual rendezvous and on line Forum are indispensible sources of information.

Fall 2010 - Gordon & Sue Brown

Here is a couple who have been around helping out at Trawler Fest and AGLCA since the beginning of time. They seemed to be everywhere help is needed. They give their time and efforts without expectation of reward.

Spring 2010 - Ted Stehle

Ted played an instrumental role in the purchase of Skipper Bob Publications by Waterway Guide Publisher Jack Dozier. At that time he took on the responsibility as editor and continues to update each guide annually. He also maintains the Skipper Bob website and spends time each day answering cruisers questions via blogs, email or phone. Ted also serves as Director of Operations for Waterway Guide.

Fall 2009 - Bob & Liz Stagg

When AGLCA hosted its first rendezvous at Joe Wheeler State Park, a couple from nearby Huntsville, AL called and asked, "How can we help?" They had not done the Loop at that point, but were inspired by stories in the newsletter. Bob and Liz started many "traditions" at AGLCA, and they continue to help "make it better" for future cruisers.

Fall 2009 - Fern Hopkins

As owners of Hoppies Marina on the Upper Mississippi River, Fern and Charles (Hoppie) know the river, the routes, and the cruisers - and everyday they work to preserve all three. Fern's "Daily Briefing" is a necessity for cruisers running southbound each fall season, as she helps calculate fuel needs, and runs down the current state of the river, locks and anchorages. Fern is essential to all boaters with her knowledge and hospitality, and has become an icon as a guardian of the river.

Spring 2009 - Tom Conrad

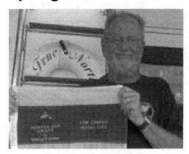

Tom is best know for his "weather musings"; reports on the AGLCA website about conditions in the Gulf of Mexico. He has spent years checking the weather for boaters to assist them in making a safe crossing from the panhandle of FL to the Tarpon Springs/Clearwater area of FL. In addition, Tom and his wife Patsy have come to the rescue more than once when a boater has been stranded in the Pensacola area.

Fall 2008 - Ken McDonald

In 2005 AGLCA members Bob and Karen Jantz, owners of Beacon Bay Marina in Penetanguishene, Ontario, began hosting summer rendezvous for AGLCA members. The highlight was a Flotilla to Killarney cruise led by Bob and Karen through the Small Craft Channel of Georgian Bay, using some little known channels. In 2007 Ken MacDonald bought Beacon Bay Marina and continued hosting an AGLCA Summer Rendezvous for many years.

Fall 2008 - Fred Myers

Fred is known best for his inland river guides, but his seminar presentations on the river system demand attention. He is always at the ready to help anyone who needs help, or wants to "pick his brain" and learn more about the river system and how to navigate them. Fred also is one of the first friends that Ron and Eva called for support in the early days of AGLCA.

Spring 2008 - Ron & Eva Stob

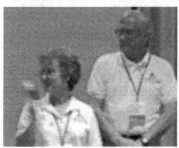

Ron and Eva are founders of the America's Great Loop Cruisers' Association (AGLCA). After completing the loop in 1994 they envisioned that future "loopers" could benefit from hearing about others experiences and that a unique social network could exist. Reaching out to friends for support they founded the AGLCA in 1999. Though not the organizations owners today, they remain deeply committed to its success.

Cruising the New York Canal System

Index